THE YALE SHAKESPEARE

Edited by

Wilbur L. Cross   Tucker Brooke

Published under the Direction
of the
Department of English, Yale University,
on the Fund
Given to the Yale University Press in 1917
by the Members of the
Kingsley Trust Association
To Commemorate the Seventy-Fifth Anniversary
of the Founding of the Society

THE MERCHANT OF VENICE

EDITED BY

WILLIAM LYON PHELPS

אורים
ותמים

LVX ET VERITAS

NEW HAVEN · YALE UNIVERSITY PRESS
LONDON · OXFORD UNIVERSITY PRESS

Copyright, 1923
By Yale University Press
Printed in the United States of America

First published, February, 1923
Second printing, March, 1938
Third printing, December, 1943
Fourth printing, March, 1946
Fifth printing, September, 1950
Sixth printing, January, 1954
Seventh printing, February, 1956
Eighth printing, November, 1957

THE JEW OF MALTA *by Christopher Marlowe*

and

THE MERCHANT OF VENICE *by William Shakespeare.*

Your Marlowe's page I close, my Shakespeare's ope.
  How welcome—after gong and cymbal's din—
The continuity, the long, slow slope,
  And vast curves of the gradual violin!

—WILLIAM WATSON.

TABLE OF CONTENTS

The facsimile opposite represents the title-page of the Elizabethan Club copy of the genuine 1600 Quarto of 'The Merchant of Venice.'

The most excellent

Historie of the *Merchant*
of *Venice*.

VVith the extreame crueltie of *Shylocke* the Iewe
towards the sayd Merchant, in cutting a iust pound
of his flesh: and the obtayning of *Portia*
by the choyse of three
chests.

As it hath beene diuers times acted by the Lord
Chamberlaine his Seruants.

Written by William Shakespeare.

AT LONDON,
Printed by *I. R.* for Thomas Heyes,
and are to be sold in Paules Church-yard, at the
signe of the Greene Dragon.
1600

DRAMATIS PERSONÆ

THE DUKE OF VENICE
MOROCHUS, *a Prince, and a Suitor to Portia*
THE PRINCE OF ARRAGON, *Suitor also to Portia*
BASSANIO, *an Italian Lord, Suitor likewise to Portia*
ANTONIO, *a Merchant of Venice*
SALARINO ⎫
SALANIO ⎬ *Gentlemen of Venice, and Companions*
GRATIANO ⎪ *with Bassanio*
LORENZO ⎭
SHYLOCK, *the rich Jew, and Father to Jessica*
TUBAL, *a Jew, Shylock's Friend*

PORTIA, *the rich Italian Lady*
NERISSA, *her waiting-Gentlewoman*
JESSICA, *Daughter to Shylock*

GOBBO, *an old man, Father to Lancelot*
LANCELOT GOBBO, *the Clown*
STEPHANO, *a Messenger*
[LEONARDO, *Servant to Bassanio*
  BALTHAZAR, *Servant to Portia*]

Gaoler and Attendants [Magnificoes of Venice, Officers
   of the Court of Justice, Servants to Portia]

[SCENE: *Alternately at Venice and at Portia's house,
             Belmont, on the mainland.*]

Dramatis Personæ; *cf. n.*

The Merchant of Venice

ACT FIRST

Scene One

[Venice.   A Street]

Enter Antonio, Salarino, and Salanio.

Ant. In sooth, I know not why I am so sad:
It wearies me; you say it wearies you;
But how I caught it, found it, or came by it,
What stuff 'tis made of, whereof it is born,   4
I am to learn;
And such a want-wit sadness makes of me,
That I have much ado to know myself.

Salar. Your mind is tossing on the ocean;   8
There, where your argosies with portly sail,—
Like signiors and rich burghers on the flood,
Or, as it were, the pageants of the sea,—
Do overpeer the petty traffickers,   12
That curtsy to them, do them reverence,
As they fly by them with their woven wings.

Salan. Believe me, sir, had I such venture forth,
The better part of my affections would   16
Be with my hopes abroad.   I should be still
Plucking the grass to know where sits the wind;
Peering in maps for ports, and piers, and roads;
And every object that might make me fear   20
Misfortune to my ventures out of doubt

---

1 sooth: *truth*   9 argosies: *large merchant ships*
11 pageants: *festival cars or floats*   12 overpeer: *tower over*
13 curtsy: *bow with the swell*   16 affections: *emotions*
17 still: *always*   21 out of doubt: *undoubtedly*

Would make me sad.

   Salar.   My wind, cooling my broth,
Would blow me to an ague, when I thought
What harm a wind too great might do at sea.   24
I should not see the sandy hour-glass run
But I should think of shallows and of flats,
And see my wealthy Andrew dock'd in sand
Vailing her high-top lower than her ribs   28
To kiss her burial. Should I go to church
And see the holy edifice of stone,
And not bethink me straight of dangerous rocks,
Which touching but my gentle vessel's side   32
Would scatter all her spices on the stream,
Enrobe the roaring waters with my silks;
And, in a word, but even now worth this,
And now worth nothing? Shall I have the thought 36
To think on this, and shall I lack the thought
That such a thing bechanc'd would make me sad?
But tell not me: I know Antonio
Is sad to think upon his merchandise.   40

   Ant. Believe me, no: I thank my fortune for it,
My ventures are not in one bottom trusted,
Nor to one place; nor is my whole estate
Upon the fortune of this present year: 44
Therefore, my merchandise makes me not sad.

   Salar. Why, then you are in love.

   Ant.   Fie, fie!

   Salar. Not in love neither? Then let's say you are
    sad,
Because you are not merry: and 'twere as easy   48
For you to laugh and leap, and say you are merry,

---

27 wealthy: *richly laden*
28 Vailing: *letting down*   high-top: *topmast*
35, 36 but even . . . nothing: *think how in a moment I may be de-*
     prived of all this wealth
36 thought: *anxiety*   38 bechanc'd: *if it happened*

Because you are not sad.   Now, by two-headed Janus,
Nature hath fram'd strange fellows in her time:
Some that will evermore peep through their eyes   52
And laugh like parrots at a bag-piper,
And other of such vinegar aspect
That they'll not show their teeth in way of smile,
Though Nestor swear the jest be laughable.   56

     Enter Bassanio, Lorenzo, and Gratiano.

     Salan. Here comes Bassanio, your most noble kins-
     man,
Gratiano, and Lorenzo.   Fare ye well:
We leave you now with better company.
     Salar. I would have stay'd till I had made you
     merry,   60
If worthier friends had not prevented me.
     Ant. Your worth is very dear in my regard.
I take it, your own business calls on you,
And you embrace the occasion to depart.   64
     Salar. Good morrow, my good lords.
     Bass. Good signiors both, when shall we laugh? say
     when?
You grow exceeding strange: must it be so?
     Salar. We'll make our leisures to attend on yours.
                [*Exeunt Salarino and Salanio.*]
     Lor. My Lord Bassanio, since you have found
     Antonio,   69
We too will leave you; but, at dinner-time,
I pray you, have in mind where we must meet.
     Bass. I will not fail you.   72
     Gra. You look not well, Signior Antonio;

50 Janus: *images of the god Janus had two faces, one laughing, one sad*
54 other: *others*
56 Nestor: *the oldest and gravest of the Greek heroes at Troy*
61 prevented: *anticipated*   62 *I regard your worthiness very highly*

You have too much respect upon the world:
They lose it that do buy it with much care:
Believe me, you are marvellously chang'd.   76

    Ant.   I hold the world but as the world, Gratiano;
A stage where every man must play a part,
And mine a sad one.

    Gra.   Let me play the fool:
With mirth and laughter let old wrinkles come,   80
And let my liver rather heat with wine
Than my heart cool with mortifying groans.
Why should a man, whose blood is warm within,
Sit like his grandsire cut in alabaster?   84
Sleep when he wakes, and creep into the jaundice
By being peevish?   I tell thee what, Antonio—
I love thee, and it is my love that speaks—
There are a sort of men whose visages   88
Do cream and mantle like a standing pond,
And do a wilful stillness entertain,
With purpose to be dress'd in an opinion
Of wisdom, gravity, profound conceit;   92
As who should say, 'I am Sir Oracle,
And when I ope my lips let no dog bark!'
O, my Antonio, I do know of these,
That therefore only are reputed wise   96
For saying nothing; when, I am very sure,
If they should speak, would almost damn those ears
Which, hearing them, would call their brothers fools.
I'll tell thee more of this another time: 100
But fish not, with this melancholy bait,
For this fool-gudgeon, this opinion.
Come, good Lorenzo.   Fare ye well awhile:

74 respect . . . world: *concern about business*   79 sad: *serious*
82 mortifying: *self-denying*
89 cream and mantle: *grow a scum*   standing: *stagnant*
91 opinion: *reputation*   92 conceit: *thought*
98 damn those ears; *cf. n.*   102 fool-gudgeon: *an easily caught fish*

I'll end my exhortation after dinner.   104

Lor. Well, we will leave you then till dinner-time.
I must be one of these same dumb-wise men,
For Gratiano never lets me speak.

Gra. Well, keep me company but two years moe, 108
Thou shalt not know the sound of thine own tongue.

Ant. Farewell: I'll grow a talker for this gear.

Gra. Thanks, i' faith; for silence is only commendable
In a neat's tongue dried and a maid not vendible.   112

                    Exit [*Gratiano with Lorenzo*].

Ant. Is that anything now?

Bass. Gratiano speaks an infinite deal of
nothing, more than any man in all Venice.   His
reasons are as two grains of wheat hid in two 116
bushels of chaff: you shall seek all day ere you
find them, and, when you have them, they are
not worth the search.

Ant. Well, tell me now, what lady is the same   120
To whom you swore a secret pilgrimage,
That you to-day promis'd to tell me of?

Bass. 'Tis not unknown to you, Antonio,
How much I have disabled mine estate,   124
By something showing a more swelling port
Than my faint means would grant continuance:
Nor do I now make moan to be abridg'd
From such a noble rate; but my chief care   128
Is, to come fairly off from the great debts
Wherein my time, something too prodigal,
Hath left me gag'd.   To you, Antonio,
I owe the most, in money and in love;   132

108 moe: *more*   110 gear: *indefinite word for business of any kind*
112 In a neat's, etc.; *cf. n.*   116 reasons: *sensible ideas*
122 That; *cf. n.*   125 By living *in a somewhat more lavish way*
127 abridg'd: *obliged to desist*   128 rate: *standard of life*
130 time: *time of life, youth*   131 gag'd: *entangled*

And from your love I have a warranty
To unburthen all my plots and purposes
How to get clear of all the debts I owe.

 Ant. I pray you, good Bassanio, let me know it; 136
And if it stand, as you yourself still do,
Within the eye of honour, be assur'd,
My purse, my person, my extremest means,
Lie all unlock'd to your occasions. 140

 Bass. In my school-days, when I had lost one shaft,
I shot his fellow of the self-same flight
The self-same way with more advised watch,
To find the other forth, and by adventuring both, 144
I oft found both. I urge this childhood proof,
Because what follows is pure innocence.
I owe you much, and, like a wilful youth,
That which I owe is lost; but if you please 148
To shoot another arrow that self way
Which you did shoot the first, I do not doubt,
As I will watch the aim, or to find both,
Or bring your latter hazard back again, 152
And thankfully rest debtor for the first.

 Ant. You know me well, and herein spend but time
To wind about my love with circumstance;
And out of doubt you do me now more wrong 156
In making question of my uttermost
Than if you had made waste of all I have:
Then do but say to me what I should do
That in your knowledge may by me be done, 160
And I am prest unto it: therefore speak.

 Bass. In Belmont is a lady richly left,

---

138 eye: *view, scope*
144 forth: *out*
149 self: *same*
154 spend but: *only waste*
161 prest: *ready*

142 flight: *power of flight, range*
146 innocence; *cf. n.*
151 or: *either*
157 question: *doubt*
162 richly left: *a wealthy heiress*

And she is fair, and, fairer than that word,
Of wondrous virtues: sometimes from her eyes   164
I did receive fair speechless messages:
Her name is Portia; nothing undervalu'd
To Cato's daughter, Brutus' Portia:
Nor is the wide world ignorant of her worth,   168
For the four winds blow in from every coast
Renowned suitors; and her sunny locks
Hang on her temples like a golden fleece;
Which makes her seat of Belmont Colchos' strond,   172
And many Jasons come in quest of her.
O my Antonio! had I but the means
To hold a rival place with one of them,
I have a mind presages me such thrift,   176
That I should questionless be fortunate.

   Ant. Thou knowest that all my fortunes are at sea;
Neither have I money, nor commodity
To raise a present sum: therefore go forth;   180
Try what my credit can in Venice do:
That shall be rack'd, even to the uttermost,
To furnish thee to Belmont, to fair Portia.
Go, presently inquire, and so will I,   184
Where money is, and I no question make
To have it of my trust or for my sake.   *Exeunt.*

163, 164 fair . . . virtues: *beautiful and accomplished*
164 sometimes: *formerly*
166 nothing undervalu'd: *in no way inferior*
167 Portia; *cf. n.*   172 Colchos'; *cf. n.*
175 hold . . . with: *make a show equal to*   176 thrift: *thriving*
182 rack'd: *strained*   184 presently: *instantly*
186 of my trust, etc.: *either on my credit or from some friend*

Scene Two

[Belmont. A Room in Portia's House]

Portia with her waiting woman Nerissa.

Por. By my troth, Nerissa, my little body is
aweary of this great world.

Ner. You would be, sweet madam, if your
miseries were in the same abundance as your 4
good fortunes are: and yet, for aught I see, they
are as sick that surfeit with too much as they
that starve with nothing. It is no mean happi-
ness therefore to be seated in the mean: 8
superfluity comes sooner by white hairs, but
competency lives longer.

Por. Good sentences and well pronounced.

Ner. They would be better if well followed.   12

Por. If to do were as easy as to know what
were good to do, chapels had been churches, and
poor men's cottages princes' palaces. It is a
good divine that follows his own instructions: I 16
can easier teach twenty what were good to be
done, than be one of the twenty to follow mine
own teaching. The brain may devise laws for
the blood, but a hot temper leaps o'er a cold 20
decree: such a hare is madness the youth, to
skip o'er the meshes of good counsel the cripple.
But this reasoning is not in the fashion to choose
me a husband. O me, the word 'choose!' I may 24
neither choose whom I would nor refuse whom
I dislike; so is the will of a living daughter
curbed by the will of a dead father. Is it not

8 seated . . . mean: *moderately endowed*
9 comes . . . by: *brings on*   11 sentences: *sentiments*

hard, Nerissa, that I cannot choose one nor 28
refuse none?

Ner. Your father was ever virtuous, and holy
men at their death have good inspirations;
therefore, the lottery that he hath devised in these 32
three chests of gold, silver, and lead, whereof
who chooses his meaning chooses you, will, no
doubt, never be chosen by any rightly but one
who you shall rightly love. But what warmth 36
is there in your affection towards any of these
princely suitors that are already come?

Por. I pray thee, over-name them, and as
thou namest them, I will describe them; and, 40
according to my description, level at my affection.

Ner. First, there is the Neapolitan prince.

Por. Ay, that's a colt indeed, for he doth
nothing but talk of his horse; and he makes it a 44
great appropriation to his own good parts that
he can shoe him himself. I am much afeard
my lady his mother played false with a smith.

Ner. Then is there the County Palatine.   48

Por. He doth nothing but frown, as who
should say, 'An you will not have me, choose.'
He hears merry tales, and smiles not: I fear he
will prove the weeping philosopher when he 52
grows old, being so full of unmannerly sadness
in his youth. I had rather be married to a
death's-head with a bone in his mouth than to
either of these. God defend me from these two! 56

Ner. How say you by the French lord,
Monsieur Le Bon?

---

34 his meaning: *the chest he meant*   41 level: *aim*
43 colt: *'brainless youth'*   45 appropriation: *peculiar merit*
48 County Palatine: *a count possessing royal privileges*
50 An: *if*   choose; *cf. n.*
52 weeping philosopher: *Heraclitus*   57 by: *concerning*

Por. God made him, and therefore let him pass
for a man. In truth, I know it is a sin to be a 60
mocker; but, he! why, he hath a horse better
than the Neapolitan's, a better bad habit of
frowning than the Count Palatine; he is every
man in no man; if a throstle sing, he falls 64
straight a-capering; he will fence with his own
shadow: if I should marry him, I should marry
twenty husbands. If he would despise me, I
would forgive him, for if he love me to madness, 68
I shall never requite him.

Ner. What say you, then, to Falconbridge,
the young baron of England?

Por. You know I say nothing to him, for he 72
understands not me, nor I him: he hath neither
Latin, French, nor Italian; and you will come
into the court and swear that I have a poor
pennyworth in the English. He is a proper 76
man's picture, but, alas! who can converse with
a dumb-show? How oddly he is suited! I think
he bought his doublet in Italy, his round hose in
France, his bonnet in Germany, and his be- 80
haviour everywhere.

Ner. What think you of the Scottish lord, his
neighbour?

Por. That he hath a neighbourly charity in 84
him, for he borrowed a box of the ear of the
Englishman, and swore he would pay him again
when he was able: I think the Frenchman became his surety and sealed under for another. 88

Ner. How like you the young German, the
Duke of Saxony's nephew?

---

64 throstle: *thrush*
76 proper: *handsome*
79 doublet: *tight-fitting coat*
87 Frenchman; *cf. n.*

74 Latin; *cf. n.*
78 suited: *dressed*
round hose: *a variety of knee-breeches*
88 sealed under: *pledged himself*

Por. Very vilely in the morning, when he is
sober, and most vilely in the afternoon, when he 92
is drunk: when he is best, he is a little worse
than a man, and when he is worst, he is little
better than a beast. An the worst fall that ever
fell, I hope I shall make shift to go without him. 96

Ner. If he should offer to choose, and choose
the right casket, you should refuse to perform
your father's will, if you should refuse to accept
him.   100

Por. Therefore, for fear of the worst, I pray
thee, set a deep glass of Rhenish wine on the
contrary casket, for, if the devil be within and
that temptation without, I know he will choose 104
it. I will do anything, Nerissa, ere I will be
married to a sponge.

Ner. You need not fear, lady, the having any
of these lords: they have acquainted me with 108
their determinations; which is, indeed, to return
to their home and to trouble you with no more
suit, unless you may be won by some other sort
than your father's imposition depending on the 112
caskets.

Por. If I live to be as old as Sibylla, I will die
as chaste as Diana, unless I be obtained by the
manner of my father's will. I am glad this 116
parcel of wooers are so reasonable, for there
is not one among them but I dote on his very
absence, and I pray God grant them a fair
departure.   120

Ner. Do you not remember, lady, in your
father's time, a Venetian, a scholar and a soldier,

111 sort: *lot*　　112 imposition: *injunction*　　114 Sibylla; *cf. n.*

that came hither in the company of the Marquis
of Montferrat?   124

Por. Yes, yes: it was Bassanio; as I think, he
was so called.

Ner. True, madam: he, of all the men that
ever my foolish eyes looked upon, was the best 128
deserving a fair lady.

Por. I remember him well, and I remember
him worthy of thy praise.

Enter a Servingman.

How now! what news?   132

Serv. The four strangers seek for you, madam,
to take their leave; and there is a forerunner
come from a fifth, the Prince of Morocco, who
brings word the prince his master will be here 136
to-night.

Por. If I could bid the fifth welcome with so
good heart as I can bid the other four farewell,
I should be glad of his approach: if he have the 140
condition of a saint and the complexion of a devil,
I had rather he should shrive me than wive me.
Come, Nerissa. Sirrah, go before.
Whiles we shut the gate upon one wooer, another
    knocks at the door.   *Exeunt.*

Scene Three

[*Venice.   A public Place*]

Enter Bassanio with Shylock the Jew.

Shy. Three thousand ducats; well?
Bass. Ay, sir, for three months.

Shy. For three months; well?

Bass. For the which, as I told you, Antonio 4
shall be bound.

Shy. Antonio shall become bound; well?

Bass. May you stead me? Will you pleasure
me? Shall I know your answer? 8

Shy. Three thousand ducats, for three
months, and Antonio bound.

Bass. Your answer to that.

Shy. Antonio is a good man. 12

Bass. Have you heard any imputation to the
contrary?

Shy. Ho, no, no, no, no: my meaning in saying
he is a good man is to have you understand me 16
that he is sufficient. Yet his means are in supposition: he hath an argosy bound to Tripolis,
another to the Indies; I understand moreover
upon the Rialto, he hath a third at Mexico, a 20
fourth for England, and other ventures he hath,
squandered abroad. But ships are but boards,
sailors but men: there be land-rats and water-
rats, land-thieves, and water-thieves,—I mean 24
pirates,—and then there is the peril of waters,
winds, and rocks. The man is, notwithstanding,
sufficient. Three thousand ducats; I think, I
may take his bond. 28

Bass. Be assured you may.

Shy. I will be assured I may; and, that I may
be assured, I will bethink me. May I speak with
Antonio? 32

Bass. If it please you to dine with us.

Shy. Yes, to smell pork; to eat of the habita-

---

7 stead: *assist*   17 supposition: *not in cash or in the bank*
20 Rialto: *the Exchange*   21 for: *bound for*
22 squandered: *scattered*

tion which your prophet the Nazarite conjured
the devil into. I will buy with you, sell with you, 36
talk with you, walk with you, and so following;
but I will not eat with you, drink with you, nor
pray with you. What news on the Rialto? Who
is he comes here?   40

Enter Antonio.

Bass. This is Signior Antonio.

Shy. [*Aside.*] How like a fawning publican he
    looks!
I hate him for he is a Christian;
But more for that in low simplicity   44
He lends out money gratis, and brings down
The rate of usance here with us in Venice.
If I can catch him once upon the hip,
I will feed fat the ancient grudge I bear him.   48
He hates our sacred nation, and he rails,
Even there where merchants most do congregate,
On me, my bargains, and my well-won thrift,
Which he calls interest. Cursed be my tribe,   52
If I forgive him!

Bass.   Shylock, do you hear?

Shy. I am debating of my present store,
And, by the near guess of my memory,
I cannot instantly raise up the gross   56
Of full three thousand ducats. What of that?
Tubal, a wealthy Hebrew of my tribe,
Will furnish me. But soft! how many months
Do you desire? [*To Antonio.*] Rest you fair, good
    signior;   60
Your worship was the last man in our mouths.

35 Nazarite; *cf. n.*   42 fawning publican: *see Luke 18. 10-14.*
44 low simplicity: *meek folly*   46 usance: *interest*
47 upon the hip: *a wrestling grip*   56 gross: *total sum*

Ant. Shylock, albeit I neither lend nor borrow
By taking nor by giving of excess,
Yet, to supply the ripe wants of my friend,   64
I'll break a custom. [*To Bassanio.*] Is he yet possess'd
How much ye would?
    Shy.   Ay, ay, three thousand ducats.
    Ant. And for three months.
    Shy. I had forgot; three months; you told me so. 68
Well then, your bond; and let me see. But hear you;
Methought you said you neither lend nor borrow
Upon advantage.
    Ant.   I do never use it.
    Shy. When Jacob graz'd his uncle Laban's sheep,—
This Jacob from our holy Abram was,   73
As his wise mother wrought in his behalf,
The third possessor: ay, he was the third,—
    Ant. And what of him? did he take interest?   76
    Shy. No; not take interest; not, as you would say,
Directly interest: mark what Jacob did.
When Laban and himself were compromis'd,
That all the eanlings which were streak'd and pied   80
Should fall as Jacob's hire, the ewes, being rank,
In end of autumn turned to the rams;
And, when the work of generation was
Between these woolly breeders in the act,   84
The skilful shepherd peel'd me certain wands,
And, in the doing of the deed of kind,
He stuck them up before the fulsome ewes,
Who, then conceiving, did in eaning time   88
Fall parti-colour'd lambs, and those were Jacob's.

---

63 excess: *interest*
65 possess'd: *informed*
79 compromis'd: *agreed*
85 peel'd me; *cf. n.*
87 fulsome: *lustful*

64 ripe: *immediate*
72 Jacob: *see Gen. 30. 37.*
80 eanlings: *new lambs*
86 kind: *nature*
89 Fall: *give birth to*

This was a way to thrive, and he was blest:
And thrift is blessing, if men steal it not.

Ant. This was a venture, sir, that Jacob serv'd for;
A thing not in his power to bring to pass,   93
But sway'd and fashion'd by the hand of heaven.
Was this inserted to make interest good?
Or is your gold and silver ewes and rams?   96

Shy. I cannot tell; I make it breed as fast:
But note me, signior.

Ant.   Mark you this, Bassanio,
The devil can cite Scripture for his purpose.
An evil soul, producing holy witness,   100
Is like a villain with a smiling cheek,
A goodly apple rotten at the heart.
O, what a goodly outside falsehood hath!

Shy. Three thousand ducats; 'tis a good round sum.
Three months from twelve, then let me see the rate. 105

Ant. Well, Shylock, shall we be beholding to you?

Shy. Signior Antonio, many a time and oft
In the Rialto you have rated me   108
About my moneys and my usances:
Still have I borne it with a patient shrug,
For sufferance is the badge of all our tribe.
You call me misbeliever, cut-throat dog,   112
And spit upon my Jewish gaberdine,
And all for use of that which is mine own.
Well then, it now appears you need my help:
Go to then; you come to me, and you say,   116
'Shylock, we would have moneys:' you say so;
You, that did void your rheum upon my beard,
And foot me as you spurn a stranger cur
Over your threshold: moneys is your suit.   120
What should I say to you? Should I not say,

106 beholding: *indebted*   113 gaberdine: *cloak or long coat*
118 void your rheum: *clear your throat*

'Hath a dog money?   Is it possible
A cur can lend three thousand ducats?' or
Shall I bend low, and in a bondman's key,   124
With bated breath, and whispering humbleness,
Say this:—
'Fair sir, you spet on me on Wednesday last;
You spurn'd me such a day; another time   128
You call'd me dog; and for these courtesies
I'll lend you thus much moneys?'

   Ant. I am as like to call thee so again,
To spet on thee again, to spurn thee too.   132
If thou wilt lend this money, lend it not
As to thy friends,—for when did friendship take
A breed for barren metal of his friend?—
But lend it rather to thine enemy;   136
Who if he break, thou mayst with better face
Exact the penalty.

   Shy.   Why, look you, how you storm!
I would be friends with you, and have your love,
Forget the shames that you have stain'd me with,   140
Supply your present wants, and take no doit
Of usance for my moneys, and you'll not hear me:
This is kind I offer.

   Bass. This were kindness.

   Shy.   This kindness will I show.   144
Go with me to a notary, seal me there
Your single bond; and, in a merry sport,
If you repay me not on such a day,
In such a place, such sum or sums as are   148
Express'd in the condition, let the forfeit
Be nominated for an equal pound
Of your fair flesh, to be cut off and taken

127 spet: *spat*
144 *Bass.; cf. n.*
150 equal: *exact*

141 doit: *Dutch coin of small value*
146 Your single: *merely your*

In what part of your body pleaseth me.   152

    Ant. Content, i' faith: I'll seal to such a bond,
And say there is much kindness in the Jew.

    Bass. You shall not seal to such a bond for me:
I'll rather dwell in my necessity.   156

    Ant. Why, fear not, man; I will not forfeit it:
Within these two months, that's a month before
This bond expires, I do expect return
Of thrice three times the value of this bond.   160

    Shy. O father Abram! what these Christians are,
Whose own hard dealings teaches them suspect
The thoughts of others.   Pray you, tell me this;
If he should break his day, what should I gain   164
By the exaction of the forfeiture?
A pound of man's flesh, taken from a man,
Is not so estimable, profitable neither,
As flesh of muttons, beefs, or goats.   I say,   168
To buy his favour, I extend this friendship:
If he will take it, so; if not, adieu;
And, for my love, I pray you wrong me not.

    Ant. Yes, Shylock, I will seal unto this bond.   172

    Shy. Then meet me forthwith at the notary's;
Give him direction for this merry bond,
And I will go and purse the ducats straight,
See to my house, left in the fearful guard   176
Of an unthrifty knave, and presently
I will be with you.   *Exit.*

    Ant.   Hie thee, gentle Jew.
This Hebrew will turn Christian: he grows kind.

    Bass. I like not fair terms and a villain's mind. 180

    Ant. Come on: in this there can be no dismay;
My ships come home a month before the day.

                                     Exeunt.

176 fearful: *fearfully insecure*

ACT SECOND

Scene One

[*Belmont.   A Room in Portia's House*]

Enter Morochus, a tawny Moor, all in white, and three or four followers accordingly, with Portia, Nerissa and their train. Flo[urish of] Cornets.

Mor. Mislike me not for my complexion,
The shadow'd livery of the burnish'd sun,
To whom I am a neighbour and near bred.
Bring me the fairest creature northward born,   4
Where Phœbus' fire scarce thaws the icicles,
And let us make incision for your love,
To prove whose blood is reddest, his or mine.
I tell thee, lady, this aspect of mine   8
Hath fear'd the valiant: by my love, I swear
The best regarded virgins of our clime
Have lov'd it too: I would not change this hue,
Except to steal your thoughts, my gentle queen.   12
Por. In terms of choice I am not solely led
By nice direction of a maiden's eyes;
Besides, the lottery of my destiny
Bars me the right of voluntary choosing: 16
But if my father had not scanted me
And hedg'd me by his wit, to yield myself
His wife who wins me by that means I told you,
Yourself, renowned prince, then stood as fair   20
As any comer I have look'd on yet
For my affection.
Mor.   Even for that I thank you:

Scene One S. d. accordingly: *in similar dress*
2 shadow'd: *dark*   7 reddest; *cf. n.*   9 fear'd: *frightened*
11, 12 I would not, etc.; *cf. n.*   14 nice: *captious*
17 scanted: *restricted*   18 wit: *intelligence*

Therefore, I pray you, lead me to the caskets
To try my fortune. By this scimitar,—   24
That slew the Sophy, and a Persian prince
That won three fields of Sultan Solyman,—
I would outstare the sternest eyes that look,
Outbrave the heart most daring on the earth,   28
Pluck the young sucking cubs from the she-bear,
Yea, mock the lion when he roars for prey,
To win thee, lady.   But, alas the while!
If Hercules and Lichas play at dice   32
Which is the better man, the greater throw
May turn by fortune from the weaker hand:
So is Alcides beaten by his page;
And so may I, blind fortune leading me,   36
Miss that which one unworthier may attain,
And die with grieving.
   Por.   You must take your chance;
And either not attempt to choose at all,
Or swear before you choose, if you choose wrong, 40
Never to speak to lady afterward
In way of marriage: therefore be advis'd.
   Mor. Nor will not: come, bring me unto my chance.
   Por. First, forward to the temple: after dinner 44
Your hazard shall be made.
   Mor.   Good fortune then!
To make me blest or cursed'st among men!
                 Cornets. Exeunt.

25 Sophy: *Shah of Persia*
26 Solyman: *He fought the Persians in 1535*
32 Lichas: *the servant of Hercules*
35 Alcides: *Alcæus was the father of Hercules' stepfather*
42 advis'd: *cautious*

Scene Two

[*Venice. A Street*]

Enter the Clown alone.

Laun. Certainly my conscience will serve me
to run from this Jew my master. The fiend is
at mine elbow, and tempts me, saying to me,
'Gobbo, Launcelot Gobbo, good Launcelot,' or 4
'good Gobbo,' or 'good Launcelot Gobbo, use
your legs, take the start, run away.' My conscience says, 'No; take heed, honest Launcelot;
take heed, honest Gobbo;' or, as aforesaid, 'honest 8
Launcelot Gobbo; do not run; scorn running
with thy heels.' Well, the most courageous fiend
bids me pack: '*Via!*' says the fiend; 'away!'
says the fiend; 'for the heavens, rouse up a brave 12
mind,' says the fiend, 'and run.' Well, my conscience, hanging about the neck of my heart, says
very wisely to me, 'My honest friend Launcelot,
being an honest man's son,'—or rather an honest 16
woman's son;—for, indeed, my father did something smack, something grow to, he had a kind
of taste;—well, my conscience says, 'Launcelot,
budge not.' 'Budge,' says the fiend. 'Budge 20
not,' says my conscience. 'Conscience,' say I,
'you counsel well;' 'fiend,' say I, 'you counsel well:'
to be ruled by my conscience, I should stay with
the Jew my master, who, God bless the mark! 24
is a kind of devil; and, to run away from the Jew,
I should be ruled by the fiend, who, saving your
reverence, is the devil himself. Certainly, the

10 with thy heels: *indignantly*   11 'Via!': *Italian, meaning "get-up"*
12 for . . . heavens: *for heaven's sake!*   18 smack, etc.; *cf. n.*
20 budge: *flinch, give ground*   24 God bless the mark; *cf. n.*
26, 27 saving your reverence: (*no offence intended!*)

Jew is the very devil incarnation; and, in my con- 28
science, my conscience is but a kind of hard conscience, to offer to counsel me to stay with the
Jew.   The fiend gives the more friendly counsel:
I will run, fiend; my heels are at your command- 32
ment; I will run.

Enter Old Gobbo, with a basket.

Gob. Master young man, you; I pray you,
which is the way to Master Jew's?

Laun. [*Aside.*] O heavens! this is my true- 36
begotten father, who, being more than sand-
blind, high-gravel blind, knows me not: I will
try confusions with him.

Gob. Master young gentleman, I pray you, 40
which is the way to Master Jew's?

Laun. Turn up on your right hand at the
next turning, but, at the next turning of all, on
your left; marry, at the very next turning, turn 44
of no hand, but turn down indirectly to the Jew's
house.

Gob. By God's sonties, 'twill be a hard way to
hit.   Can you tell me whether one Launcelot, 48
that dwells with him, dwell with him or no?

Laun. Talk you of young Master Launcelot?
[*Aside.*] Mark me now; now will I raise the
waters.   Talk you of young Master Launcelot? 52

Gob. No master, sir, but a poor man's son:
his father, though I say it, is an honest, exceeding poor man, and, God be thanked, well to
live.   56

Laun. Well, let his father be what a' will, we
talk of young Master Launcelot.

Gob. Your worship's friend, and Launcelot, sir.   60

Laun. But I pray you, *ergo,* old man, *ergo,* I beseech you, talk you of young Master Launcelot?

Gob. Of Launcelot, an 't please your mastership.   64

Laun. Ergo, Master Launcelot. Talk not of Master Launcelot, father; for the young gentleman,—according to Fates and Destinies and such odd sayings, the Sisters Three and such branches 68 of learning,—is, indeed, deceased; or, as you would say in plain terms, gone to heaven.

Gob. Marry, God forbid! the boy was the very staff of my age, my very prop.   72

Laun. [*Aside.*] Do I look like a cudgel or a hovel-post, a staff or a prop? Do you know me, father?

Gob. Alack the day! I know you not, young 76 gentleman: but I pray you, tell me, is my boy,— God rest his soul!—alive or dead?

Laun. Do you not know me, father?

Gob. Alack, sir, I am sand-blind; I know you 80 not.

Laun. Nay, indeed, if you had your eyes, you might fail of the knowing me: it is a wise father that knows his own child. Well, old man, 84 I will tell you news of your son. Give me your blessing; truth will come to light; murder cannot be hid long; a man's son may, but, in the end, truth will out.   88

Gob. Pray you, sir, stand up. I am sure you are not Launcelot, my boy.

Laun. Pray you, let's have no more fooling

about it, but give me your blessing: I am 92
Launcelot, your boy that was, your son that is,
your child that shall be.

Gob. I cannot think you are my son.

Laun. I know not what I shall think of that; 96
but I am Launcelot, the Jew's man, and I am
sure Margery your wife is my mother.

Gob. Her name is Margery, indeed: I'll be
sworn, if thou be Launcelot, thou art mine own 100
flesh and blood. Lord worshipped might he be!
what a beard hast thou got! thou hast got more
hair on thy chin than Dobbin my phill-horse has
on his tail. 104

Laun. It should seem then that Dobbin's tail
grows backward: I am sure he had more hair on
his tail than I have on my face, when I last saw
him. 108

Gob. Lord! how art thou changed. How dost
thou and thy master agree? I have brought him
a present. How 'gree you now?

Laun. Well, well: but, for mine own part, as 112
I have set up my rest to run away, so I will not
rest till I have run some ground. My master's a
very Jew: give him a present! give him a halter:
I am famished in his service: you may tell every 116
finger I have with my ribs. Father, I am glad
you are come: give me your present to one
Master Bassanio, who, indeed, gives rare new
liveries. If I serve not him, I will run as far 120
as God has any ground. O rare fortune! here

101 Lord . . . be: *Praise the Lord!*
102 what a beard; *cf. n.*   103 phill-horse: *shaft-horse*
113 set up my rest: *staked all, resolved absolutely (card-game term)*
116 tell: *count; cf. n.*
121 God has any ground: *He had little in Venice*

comes the man: to him, father; for I am a Jew,
if I serve the Jew any longer.

Enter Bassanio, with a follower [Leonardo] or two.

Bass. You may do so; but let it be so hasted 124
that supper be ready at the farthest by five
of the clock. See these letters delivered; put
the liveries to making; and desire Gratiano to
come anon to my lodging.   [*Exit a Servant.*] 128

Laun. To him, father.

Gob. God bless your worship!

Bass. Gramercy! wouldst thou aught with
me?   132

Gob. Here's my son, sir, a poor boy,—

Laun. Not a poor boy, sir, but the rich
Jew's man; that would, sir,—as my father shall
specify,—   136

Gob. He hath a great infection, sir, as one
would say, to serve—

Laun. Indeed, the short and the long is, I serve
the Jew, and have a desire, as my father shall 140
specify,—

Gob. His master and he, saving your worship's reverence, are scarce cater-cousins,—

Laun. To be brief, the very truth is that the 144
Jew having done me wrong, doth cause me,—
as my father, being, I hope, an old man, shall
frutify unto you,—

Gob. I have here a dish of doves that I 148
would bestow upon your worship, and my suit
is,—

Laun. In very brief, the suit is impertinent

131 Gramercy: *grand merci, many thanks*
143 cater-cousins: *speaking acquaintances*
147 frutify: *i.e., notify* (?)   151 impertinent: *i.e., pertinent, relating*

to myself, as your worship shall know by this 152
honest old man; and, though I say it, though
old man, yet poor man, my father.

Bass. One speak for both. What would you?

Laun. Serve you, sir.   156

Gob. That is the very defect of the matter,
sir.

Bass. I know thee well; thou hast obtain'd thy suit:
Shylock thy master spoke with me this day,   160
And hath preferr'd thee, if it be preferment
To leave a rich Jew's service, to become
The follower of so poor a gentleman.

Laun. The old proverb is very well parted 164
between my master Shylock and you, sir: you
have the grace of God, sir, and he hath enough.

Bass. Thou speak'st it well. Go, father, with thy
son.

Take leave of thy old master, and inquire   168
My lodging out. [*To his followers.*] Give him a livery
More guarded than his fellows': see it done.

Laun. Father, in. I cannot get a service, no;
I have ne'er a tongue in my head. Well, [*Look-* 172
ing on his palm] if any man in Italy have a
fairer table which doth offer to swear upon a
book, I shall have good fortune. Go to; here's
a simple line of life: here's a small trifle of wives: 176
alas! fifteen wives is nothing: a 'leven widows and
nine maids is a simple coming-in for one man;
and then to 'scape drowning thrice, and to be in
peril of my life with the edge of a feather-bed; 180
here are simple 'scapes. Well, if Fortune be a
woman, she's a good wench for this gear. Father,

161 preferr'd: *recommended*   preferment: *advancement*
164 The old proverb; *cf. n.*   170 guarded: *adorned with facings*
174 table; *cf. n.*   178 simple coming-in: *small inheritance*

come; I'll take my leave of the Jew in the
twinkling of an eye.   184

                 Exit Clown [*with Old Gobbo*].
  Bass. I pray thee, good Leonardo, think on this:
These things being bought, and orderly bestow'd,
Return in haste, for I do feast to-night
My best-esteem'd acquaintance: hie thee, go.   188
  Leon. My best endeavours shall be done herein.

             Enter Gratiano.

  Gra. Where is your master?
  Leon.   Yonder, sir, he walks.
                        [*Exit.*]

  Gra. Signior Bassanio!—
  Bass. Gratiano!   192
  Gra. I have a suit to you.
  Bass.   You have obtain'd it.
  Gra. You must not deny me: I must go with you to
    Belmont.
  Bass. Why, then you must.   But hear thee,
    Gratiano;
Thou art too wild, too rude and bold of voice;   196
Parts that become thee happily enough,
And in such eyes as ours appear not faults;
But where thou art not known, why, there they show
Something too liberal.   Pray thee, take pain   200
To allay with some cold drops of modesty
Thy skipping spirit, lest, through thy wild behaviour,
I be misconstru'd in the place I go to,
And lose my hopes.
  Gra.   Signior Bassanio, hear me: 204
If I do not put on a sober habit,
Talk with respect, and swear but now and then,

188 hie thee: *hurry up*   200 liberal: *unrestrained*
205 habit: *behavior*

Wear prayer-books in my pocket, look demurely,
Nay more, while grace is saying, hood mine eyes   208
Thus with my hat, and sigh, and say 'amen;'
Use all the observance of civility,
Like one well studied in a sad ostent
To please his grandam, never trust me more.   212

    Bass. Well, we shall see your bearing.

    Gra. Nay, but I bar to-night; you shall not gauge me
By what we do to-night.

    Bass.   No, that were pity:
I would entreat you rather to put on   216
Your boldest suit of mirth, for we have friends
That purpose merriment.   But fare you well:
I have some business.

    Gra. And I must to Lorenzo and the rest;   220
But we will visit you at supper-time.   *Exeunt.*

Scene Three

[*The Same.   A Room in Shylock's House*]

Enter Jessica and the Clown.

    Jes. I am sorry thou wilt leave my father so:
Our house is hell, and thou, a merry devil,
Didst rob it of some taste of tediousness.
But fare thee well; there is a ducat for thee: 4
And, Launcelot, soon at supper shalt thou see
Lorenzo, who is thy new master's guest:
Give him this letter; do it secretly;
And so farewell: I would not have my father   8

208 hood: *hats were worn at meals, but removed during grace*
211 studied: *rehearsed*   sad ostent: *serious appearance*
3 taste: *small bit*

See me in talk with thee.

    Laun. Adieu! tears exhibit my tongue.   Most
beautiful pagan, most sweet Jew! If a Christian
did not play the knave and get thee, I am much 12
deceived.   But, adieu! these foolish drops do
somewhat drown my manly spirit: adieu!   *Exit.*

    Jes. Farewell, good Launcelot.

Alack, what heinous sin is it in me   16
To be asham'd to be my father's child!
But though I am a daughter to his blood,
I am not to his manners.   O Lorenzo!
If thou keep promise, I shall end this strife,   20
Become a Christian, and thy loving wife.   *Exit.*

Scene Four

[*The Same.   A Street*]

Enter Gratiano, Lorenzo, Salarino, and Salanio.

    Lor. Nay, we will slink away in supper-time,
Disguise us at my lodging, and return
All in an hour.

    Gra. We have not made good preparation.   4

    Salar. We have not spoke us yet of torch-bearers.

    Salan. 'Tis vile, unless it may be quaintly order'd,
And better, in my mind, not undertook.

    Lor. 'Tis now but four o'clock: we have two hours 8
To furnish us.

Enter Launcelot, with a letter.

          Friend Launcelot, what's the news?

    Laun. An it shall please you to break up this,
it shall seem to signify.

---

10 exhibit, etc.: *express what my tongue would say*
5 spoke us of: *ordered*   6 quaintly: *ingeniously*
10 break up: *break the seals of*

Lor. I know the hand: in faith, 'tis a fair hand;   12
And whiter than the paper it writ on
Is the fair hand that writ.

Gra.   Love news, in faith.

Laun. By your leave, sir.

Lor. Whither goest thou?   16

   Laun. Marry, sir, to bid my old master, the
Jew, to sup to-night with my new master, the
Christian.

Lor. Hold here, take this: tell gentle Jessica   20
I will not fail her; speak it privately.
Go, gentlemen,   [*Exit Clown.*
Will you prepare you for this masque to-night?
I am provided of a torch-bearer.   24

Salar. Ay, marry, I'll be gone about it straight.

Salan. And so will I.

Lor.   Meet me and Gratiano
At Gratiano's lodging some hour hence.

Salar. 'Tis good we do so.   28

                    Exit [*with Salanio*].

Gra. Was not that letter from fair Jessica?

Lor. I must needs tell thee all.   She hath directed
How I shall take her from her father's house;
What gold and jewels she is furnish'd with;   32
What page's suit she hath in readiness.
If e'er the Jew her father come to heaven,
It will be for his gentle daughter's sake;
And never dare misfortune cross her foot,   36
Unless she do it under this excuse,
That she is issue to a faithless Jew.
Come, go with me: peruse this as thou goest.
Fair Jessica shall be my torch-bearer.   40

                    Exit [*with Gratiano*].

---

38 faithless: *without Christian faith*

Scene Five

[The Same.　Before Shylock's House]

Enter Jew and his man that was the Clown.

Shy. Well, thou shalt see, thy eyes shall be thy
　judge,
The difference of old Shylock and Bassanio:—
What, Jessica!—thou shalt not gormandize,
As thou hast done with me;—What, Jessica!—　　4
And sleep and snore, and rend apparel out—
Why, Jessica, I say!

Laun.　　　　　　　　Why, Jessica!

Shy. Who bids thee call? I do not bid thee call.

　Laun. Your worship was wont to tell me that　8
I could do nothing without bidding.

Enter Jessica.

Jes. Call you? What is your will?

Shy. I am bid forth to supper, Jessica:
There are my keys. But wherefore should I go?　　12
I am not bid for love; they flatter me:
But yet I'll go in hate, to feed upon
The prodigal Christian. Jessica, my girl,
Look to my house. I am right loath to go:　　16
There is some ill a-brewing towards my rest
For I did dream of money-bags to-night.

　Laun. I beseech you, sir, go: my young
master doth expect your reproach.　　20

Shy. So do I his.

　Laun. And they have conspired together: I
will not say you shall see a masque; but if you
do, then it was not for nothing that my nose fell　24

5 rend: *wear*　　　　　　　18 to-night: *last night*
24 nose, etc.: *a sign of bad luck, universally believed*

a-bleeding on Black-Monday last, at six o'clock
i' the morning, falling out that year on Ash-
Wednesday was four year in the afternoon.

Shy. What! are there masques? Hear you me,
    Jessica: 28
Lock up my doors; and when you hear the drum,
And the vile squealing of the wry-neck'd fife,
Clamber not you up to the casements then,
Nor thrust your head into the public street   32
To gaze on Christian fools with varnish'd faces,
But stop my house's ears, I mean my casements;
Let not the sound of shallow foppery enter
My sober house.   By Jacob's staff I swear   36
I have no mind of feasting forth to-night;
But I will go.   Go you before me, sirrah;
Say I will come.

    Laun. I will go before, sir.   Mistress, look out 40
  at window, for all this;
        There will come a Christian by,
        Will be worth a Jewess' eye.

                  [*Exit Launcelot.*]

Shy. What says that fool of Hagar's offspring, ha?

Jes. His words were, 'Farewell, mistress;' nothing
    else.   45

Shy. The patch is kind enough, but a huge feeder;
Snail-slow in profit, and he sleeps by day
More than the wild cat: drones hive not with me;   48
Therefore I part with him, and part with him

25 Black-Monday: *Easter Monday*
26, 27 falling out, etc.: *mere nonsense*
30 wry-neck'd: *played with the head twisted*
33 with varnish'd faces: *wearing painted masks* (or perhaps *painted*
    with cosmetics)
35 foppery: *folly*   36 Jacob's staff: *cf. Gen. 32. 10; Heb. 11. 21*
37 forth: *out*   43 Jewess' eye; *cf. n.*   44 Hagar's; *cf. Gen. 16.*
46 patch: *the dress of fools, hence term of contempt; cf. cross-patch*
47 profit: *acquired proficiency, training*

To one that I would have him help to waste
His borrow'd purse. Well, Jessica, go in:
Perhaps I will return immediately: 52
Do as I bid you; shut doors after you:
'Fast bind, fast find,'
A proverb never stale in thrifty mind.   *Exit.*

Jes. Farewell; and if my fortune be not crost,   56
I have a father, you a daughter, lost.   *Exit.*

Scene Six

[*The Same*]

Enter the Maskers, Gratiano and Salarino.

Gra. This is the penthouse under which Lorenzo
Desir'd us to make stand.
Salar.   His hour is almost past.
Gra. And it is marvel he out-dwells his hour,
For lovers ever run before the clock.   4
Salar. O! ten times faster Venus' pigeons fly
To seal love's bonds new-made, than they are wont
To keep obliged faith unforfeited!
Gra. That ever holds: who riseth from a feast   8
With that keen appetite that he sits down?
Where is the horse that doth untread again
His tedious measures with the unbated fire
That he did pace them first? All things that are,   12
Are with more spirit chased than enjoy'd.
How like a younker or a prodigal
The scarfed bark puts from her native bay,
Hugg'd and embraced by the strumpet wind!   16
How like the prodigal doth she return,

1 penthouse: *an attached shed, lean-to*
5 Venus' pigeons: *doves drew her chariot*   7 obliged: *contracted*
10 untread: *retrace*   14 younker: *eager youth*   15 scarfed; *cf. n.*

With over-weather'd ribs and ragged sails,
Lean, rent, and beggar'd by the strumpet wind!
    Salar. Here comes Lorenzo: more of this hereafter.

Enter Lorenzo.

    Lor. Sweet friends, your patience for my long
        abode;   21
Not I, but my affairs, have made you wait:
When you shall please to play the thieves for wives,
I'll watch as long for you then.   Approach;   24
Here dwells my father Jew.   Ho! who's within?

[Enter] Jessica above [in boy's clothes].

    Jes. Who are you?   Tell me, for more certainty,
Albeit I'll swear that I do know your tongue.
    Lor. Lorenzo, and thy love.   28
    Jes. Lorenzo, certain; and my love indeed,
For whom love I so much?   And now who knows
But you, Lorenzo, whether I am yours?
    Lor. Heaven and thy thoughts are witness that thou
        art.   32
    Jes. Here, catch this casket; it is worth the pains.
I am glad 'tis night, you do not look on me,
For I am much asham'd of my exchange;
But love is blind, and lovers cannot see   36
The pretty follies that themselves commit;
For if they could, Cupid himself would blush
To see me thus transformed to a boy.
    Lor. Descend, for you must be my torch-bearer.   40
    Jes. What! must I hold a candle to my shames?
They in themselves, good sooth, are too-too light.
Why, 'tis an office of discovery, love,

21 abode: *delay*   31 yours: *i.e., whether you love me*
35 exchange: *transformation*   43 discovery: *revealing*

And I should be obscur'd.

    Lor.   So are you, sweet,   44

Even in the lovely garnish of a boy.

But come at once;

For the close night doth play the runaway,

And we are stay'd for at Bassanio's feast.   48

    Jes. I will make fast the doors, and gild myself

With some more ducats, and be with you straight.

                      [Exit above.]

    Gra. Now, by my hood, a Gentile, and no Jew.

    Lor. Beshrew me, but I love her heartily;   52

For she is wise, if I can judge of her,

And fair she is, if that mine eyes be true,

And true she is, as she hath prov'd herself;

And therefore, like herself, wise, fair, and true,   56

Shall she be placed in my constant soul.

              Enter Jessica.

What art thou come? On, gentlemen; away!

Our masquing mates by this time for us stay.

           Exit [with Jessica and Salarino].

              Enter Antonio.

    Ant. Who's there?   60

    Gra. Signior Antonio!

    Ant. Fie, fie, Gratiano! where are all the rest?

'Tis nine o'clock; our friends all stay for you.

No masque to-night: the wind is come about;   64

Bassanio presently will go aboard:

I have sent twenty out to seek for you.

    Gra. I am glad on 't: I desire no more delight

Than to be under sail and gone to-night.   68

                  Exeunt.

45 garnish: *dress*   47 close: *secret*
52 Beshrew: *curse, a mild oath*

Scene Seven

[*Belmont.   A Room in Portia's House*]

Enter Portia, with Morocco, and both their Trains.

Por. Go, draw aside the curtains, and discover
The several caskets to this noble prince.
Now make your choice.

    Mor. The first, of gold, which this inscription bears:
Who chooseth me shall gain what many men desire.   5
The second, silver, which this promise carries:
Who chooseth me shall get as much as he deserves.
This third, dull lead, with warning all as blunt: 8
Who chooseth me must give and hazard all he hath.
How shall I know if I do choose the right?

    Por. The one of them contains my picture, prince:
If you choose that, then I am yours withal.   12

    Mor. Some god direct my judgment! Let me see:
I will survey the inscriptions back again:
What says this leaden casket?
Who chooseth me must give and hazard all he hath.   16
Must give: For what? for lead? hazard for lead?
This casket threatens.   Men that hazard all
Do it in hope of fair advantages:
A golden mind stoops not to shows of dross;   20
I'll then nor give nor hazard aught for lead.
What says the silver with her virgin hue?
Who chooseth me shall get as much as he deserves.
As much as he deserves! Pause there, Morocco,   24
And weigh thy value with an even hand.
If thou be'st rated by thy estimation,
Thou dost deserve enough; and yet enough

---

1 discover: *reveal*   8 all as blunt: *equally blunt*
12 withal: *therewith*   25 with an even hand: *impartially*
26 rated . . . estimation: *valued according to thy worth*

May not extend so far as to the lady: 28
And yet to be afeard of my deserving
Were but a weak disabling of myself.
As much as I deserve! Why, that's the lady:
I do in birth deserve her, and in fortunes,   32
In graces, and in qualities of breeding;
But more than these, in love I do deserve.
What if I stray'd no further, but chose here?
Let's see once more this saying grav'd in gold: 36
Who chooseth me shall gain what many men desire.
Why, that's the lady: all the world desires her;
From the four corners of the earth they come,
To kiss this shrine, this mortal-breathing saint: 40
The Hyrcanian deserts and the vasty wilds
Of wide Arabia are as throughfares now
For princes to come view fair Portia:
The watery kingdom, whose ambitious head   44
Spits in the face of heaven, is no bar
To stop the foreign spirits, but they come,
As o'er a brook, to see fair Portia.
One of these three contains her heavenly picture.   48
Is 't like that lead contains her? 'Twere damnation
To think so base a thought: it were too gross
To rib her cerecloth in the obscure grave.
Or shall I think in silver she's immur'd,   52
Being ten times undervalu'd to tried gold?
O sinful thought! Never so rich a gem
Was set in worse than gold. They have in England
A coin that bears the figure of an angel   56
Stamped in gold, but that's insculp'd upon;

30 disabling: *disparagement*   33 *In natural and acquired advantages*
36 grav'd: *engraved*   40 shrine: *image*
41 Hyrcanian: *south of the Caspian Sea*
42 throughfares: *thoroughfares*
51 rib: *enclose*   cerecloth: *winding sheet*
53 undervalu'd: *inferior in value*   56 angel: *gold coin worth 10s.*
57 insculp'd upon: *engraved on the outside*

But here an angel in a golden bed
Lies all within. Deliver me the key:
Here do I choose, and thrive I as I may!   60
   Por. There, take it, prince; and if my form lie there
Then I am yours.

                    [*He unlocks the golden casket.*]
   Mor.   O hell! what have we here?
A carrion Death, within whose empty eye
There is a written scroll. I'll read the writing.   64

            'All that glisters is not gold;
               Often have you heard that told:
               Many a man his life hath sold
               But my outside to behold: 68
               Gilded tombs do worms infold.
               Had you been as wise as bold,
               Young in limbs, in judgment old,
               Your answer had not been inscroll'd: 72
               Fare you well; your suit is cold.'

   Cold, indeed; and labour lost:
Then, farewell, heat, and welcome, frost!
Portia, adieu. I have too griev'd a heart   76
To take a tedious leave: thus losers part.

                    Exit [*with his Train*].
   Por. A gentle riddance. Draw the curtains: go.
Let all of his complexion choose me so.

                    Flo[*urish of*] *Cornets. Exeunt.*

                    Scene Eight

                    [*Venice. A Street*]

                    Enter Salarino and Salanio.

   Salar. Why, man, I saw Bassanio under sail:
With him is Gratiano gone along;

And in their ship I'm sure Lorenzo is not.

   Salan. The villain Jew with outcries rais'd the duke,
Who went with him to search Bassanio's ship.   5

   Salar. He came too late, the ship was under sail:
But there the duke was given to understand
That in a gondola were seen together   8
Lorenzo and his amorous Jessica.
Besides, Antonio certified the duke
They were not with Bassanio in his ship.

   Salan. I never heard a passion so confus'd,   12
So strange, outrageous, and so variable,
As the dog Jew did utter in the streets:
'My daughter! O my ducats! O my daughter!
Fled with a Christian! O my Christian ducats!   16
Justice! the law! my ducats, and my daughter!
A sealed bag, two sealed bags of ducats,
Of double ducats, stol'n from me by my daughter!
And jewels! two stones, two rich and precious stones,
Stol'n by my daughter! Justice! find the girl!   21
She hath the stones upon her, and the ducats.'

   Salar. Why, all the boys in Venice follow him,
Crying, his stones, his daughter, and his ducats.   24

   Salan. Let good Antonio look he keep his day,
Or he shall pay for this.

   Salar.   Marry, well remember'd.
I reason'd with a Frenchman yesterday,
Who told me,—in the narrow seas that part   28
The French and English,—there miscarried
A vessel of our country richly fraught.
I thought upon Antonio when he told me,
And wish'd in silence that it were not his.   32

   Salan. You were best to tell Antonio what you hear;
Yet do not suddenly, for it may grieve him.

12 passion: *sorrow*   27 reason'd: *talked*

Salar. A kinder gentleman treads not the earth.
I saw Bassanio and Antonio part: 36
Bassanio told him he would make some speed
Of his return: he answer'd 'Do not so;
Slubber not business for my sake, Bassanio,
But stay the very riping of the time; 40
And for the Jew's bond which he hath of me,
Let it not enter in your mind of love:
Be merry, and employ your chiefest thoughts
To courtship and such fair ostents of love 44
As shall conveniently become you there:'
And even there, his eye being big with tears,
Turning his face, he put his hand behind him,
And with affection wondrous sensible 48
He wrung Bassanio's hand; and so they parted.
   Salan. I think he only loves the world for him.
I pray thee, let us go and find him out,
And quicken his embraced heaviness 52
With some delight or other.
   Salar.   Do we so.

                                        Exeunt.

Scene Nine

[*Belmont.   A Room in Portia's House*]

Enter Nerissa, and a Servitor.

Ner. Quick, quick, I pray thee; draw the curtain
      straight:
The Prince of Arragon hath ta'en his oath,
And comes to his election presently.

39 Slubber: *spoil by scamping*   42 mind of love: *loving mind*
44 ostents: *displays*   45 conveniently: *properly*
48 sensible: *charged with feeling*
52 embraced heaviness: *the sorrow that he so clings to*
3 election: *choice*

Enter Arragon, his train, and Portia.   Flor[ish of]
Cornets.

Por. Behold, there stand the caskets, noble prince:
If you choose that wherein I am contain'd,   5
Straight shall our nuptial rites be solemniz'd;
But if you fail, without more speech, my lord,
You must be gone from hence immediately.   8

Ar. I am enjoin'd by oath to observe three things:
First, never to unfold to any one
Which casket 'twas I chose; next, if I fail
Of the right casket, never in my life   12
To woo a maid in way of marriage;
Lastly,
If I do fail in fortune of my choice,
Immediately to leave you and be gone.   16

Por. To these injunctions every one doth swear
That comes to hazard for my worthless self.

Ar. And so have I address'd me.   Fortune now
To my heart's hope! Gold, silver, and base lead.   20
Who chooseth me must give and hazard all he hath:
You shall look fairer, ere I give or hazard.
What says the golden chest? ha! let me see:
Who chooseth me shall gain what many men desire.   24
What many men desire! that 'many' may be meant
By the fool multitude, that choose by show,
Not learning more than the fond eye doth teach,
Which pries not to the interior, but, like the martlet, 28
Builds in the weather on the outward wall,
Even in the force and road of casualty.
I will not choose what many men desire,

18 comes to hazard: *incurs risk*   19 address'd me: *prepared myself*
26 By: *for*   27 fond: *foolish*
28 martlet: *martin (see Macbeth I. vi. 4)*
30 force and road: *'in vi et via,' i.e., where accident occurs with the
greatest violence and frequency*

Because I will not jump with common spirits   32
And rank me with the barbarous multitude.
Why, then to thee, thou silver treasure-house;
Tell me once more what title thou dost bear:
Who chooseth me shall get as much as he deserves.   36
And well said too; for who shall go about
To cozen fortune and be honourable
Without the stamp of merit?   Let none presume
To wear an undeserved dignity.   40
O! that estates, degrees, and offices
Were not deriv'd corruptly, and that clear honour
Were purchas'd by the merit of the wearer.
How many then should cover that stand bare;   44
How many be commanded that command;
How much low peasantry would then be glean'd
From the true seed of honour; and how much honour
Pick'd from the chaff and ruin of the times   48
To be new varnish'd! Well, but to my choice:
Who chooseth me shall get as much as he deserves.
I will assume desert.   Give me a key for this,
And instantly unlock my fortunes here.   52

　　　　　　　[*He opens the silver casket.*]

　Por. Too long a pause for that which you find there.
　Ar. What's here? the portrait of a blinking idiot,
Presenting me a schedule!   I will read it.
How much unlike art thou to Portia!   56
How much unlike my hopes and my deservings!
Who chooseth me shall have as much as he deserves.
Did I deserve no more than a fool's head?
Is that my prize? are my deserts no better?   60

32 jump: *agree*　　33 rank me: *class myself*　　37 go about: *undertake*
38 cozen: *cheat*　　　　honourable: *worshipful, honored*
41 estates: *status, position*　　degrees: *ranks*　　42 deriv'd: *inherited*
44 cover: *wear their hats (in token of social dignity)*
47 true . . . honour: *scions of the great*
48 chaff and ruin: *riff-raff*　　　　　　　　51 assume: *claim*

Por. To offend, and judge, are distinct offices,
And of opposed natures.

    Ar.   What is here?

> 'The fire seven times tried this:
> Seven times tried that judgment is   64
> That did never choose amiss.
> Some there be that shadows kiss;
> Such have but a shadow's bliss:
> There be fools alive, I wis,   68
> Silver'd o'er; and so was this.
> Take what wife you will to bed,
> I will ever be your head:
> So be gone, sir: you are sped.'   72

> Still more fool I shall appear
> By the time I linger here:
> With one fool's head I came to woo,
> But I go away with two.   76
> Sweet, adieu. I'll keep my oath,
> Patiently to bear my wroth.

                      [Exit Arragon with his Train.]

Por. Thus hath the candle sing'd the moth.
O, these deliberate fools! when they do choose,   80
They have the wisdom by their wit to lose.

    Ner. The ancient saying is no heresy:
'Hanging and wiving goes by destiny.'

    Por. Come, draw the curtain, Nerissa.   84

Enter Messenger.

    Mes. Where is my lady?

    Por.   Here; what would my lord?

    Mes. Madam, there is alighted at your gate
A young Venetian, one that comes before

---

61 To offend, etc.: *the criminal need not judge his own case*
68 I wis: *corruption of 'gewis,' certainly*   85 my lord; *cf. n.*

To signify the approaching of his lord;   88
From whom he bringeth sensible regreets,
To wit,—besides commends and courteous breath,—
Gifts of rich value.   Yet I have not seen
So likely an embassador of love.   92
A day in April never came so sweet,
To show how costly summer was at hand,
As this fore-spurrer comes before his lord.

  Por. No more, I pray thee: I am half afeard   96
Thou wilt say anon he is some kin to thee,
Thou spend'st such high-day wit in praising him.
Come, come, Nerissa; for I long to see
Quick Cupid's post that comes so mannerly.   100

  Ner. Bassanio, lord Love, if thy will it be!

                                    Exeunt.

ACT THIRD

Scene One

[Venice.   A Street]

Enter Salanio and Salarino.

  Salan. Now, what news on the Rialto?

  Salar. Why, yet it lives there unchecked that
Antonio hath a ship of rich lading wracked on
the narrow seas; the Goodwins, I think they call 4
the place; a very dangerous flat, and fatal, where
the carcasses of many a tall ship lie buried, as
they say, if my gossip Report be an honest
woman of her word.   8

89 sensible: *substantial, meaning his gifts*   regreets: *greetings*
92 likely: *promising*
98 high-day: *holiday, meaning ornate, dressed for holiday*
3 wracked: *wrecked*   4 narrow seas: *English Channel*

Salan. I would she were as lying a gossip in that as ever knapped ginger, or made her neighbours believe she wept for the death of a third husband. But it is true,—without any slips of 12 prolixity or crossing the plain highway of talk, —that the good Antonio, the honest Antonio,— O, that I had a title good enough to keep his name company!—   16

Salar. Come, the full stop.

Salan. Ha! what sayst thou? Why, the end is, he hath lost a ship.

Salar. I would it might prove the end of his 20 losses.

Salan. Let me say 'amen' betimes, lest the devil cross my prayer, for here he comes in the likeness of a Jew.   24

Enter Shylock.

How now, Shylock! what news among the merchants?

Shy. You knew, none so well, none so well as you, of my daughter's flight.   28

Salar. That's certain: I, for my part, knew the tailor that made the wings she flew withal.

Salan. And Shylock, for his own part, knew the bird was fledged; and then it is the com- 32 plexion of them all to leave the dam.

Shy. She is damned for it.

Salar. That's certain, if the devil may be her judge.   36

Shy. My own flesh and blood to rebel!

Salan. Out upon it, old carrion! rebels it at these years?

---

10 knapped: *munched (pronounce the 'k')*   30 withal: *with; cf. n.*
32 complexion: *disposition*

Shy. I say my daughter is my flesh and 40 blood.

Salar. There is more difference between thy flesh and hers than between jet and ivory; more between your bloods than there is between red 44 wine and Rhenish. But tell us, do you hear whether Antonio have had any loss at sea or no?

Shy. There I have another bad match: a 48 bankrupt, a prodigal, who dare scarce show his head on the Rialto; a beggar, that was used to come so smug upon the mart; let him look to his bond: he was wont to call me usurer; let him look 52 to his bond: he was wont to lend money for a Christian courtesy; let him look to his bond.

Salar. Why, I am sure, if he forfeit thou wilt not take his flesh: what's that good for? 56

Shy. To bait fish withal: if it feed nothing else, it will feed my revenge. He hath disgraced me, and hindered me half a million, laughed at my losses, mocked at my gains, scorned my 60 nation, thwarted my bargains, cooled my friends, heated mine enemies; and what's his reason? I am a Jew. Hath not a Jew eyes? hath not a Jew hands, organs, dimensions, senses, affec- 64 tions, passions? fed with the same food, hurt with the same weapons, subject to the same diseases, healed by the same means, warmed and cooled by the same winter and summer, as a 68 Christian is? If you prick us, do we not bleed? if you tickle us, do we not laugh? if you poison us, do we not die? and if you wrong us, shall we not revenge? If we are like you in the rest, we 72 will resemble you in that. If a Jew wrong a

Christian, what is his humility? Revenge. If a
Christian wrong a Jew, what should his sufferance
be by Christian example? Why, revenge. The 76
villainy you teach me I will execute, and it shall
go hard but I will better the instruction.

Enter a man from Antonio.

Man. Gentlemen, my master Antonio is at his
house, and desires to speak with you both.   80

Salar. We have been up and down to seek
him.

Enter Tubal.

Salan. Here comes another of the tribe: a
third cannot be matched, unless the devil him- 84
self turn Jew.

*Exeunt Gentlemen [i.e. Salanio, Salarino,
and Antonio's man].*

Shy. How now, Tubal! what news from Genoa? Hast thou found my daughter?

Tub. I often came where I did hear of her, 88
but cannot find her.

Shy. Why there, there, there, there! a diamond
gone, cost me two thousand ducats in Frankfort!
The curse never fell upon our nation till now; I 92
never felt it till now: two thousand ducats in
that; and other precious, precious jewels. I
would my daughter were dead at my foot, and
the jewels in her ear! would she were hearsed at 96
my foot, and the ducats in her coffin! No news
of them? Why, so: and I know not what's spent
in the search: Why thou—loss upon loss! the
thief gone with so much, and so much to find the 100
thief; and no satisfaction, no revenge: nor no ill

luck stirring but what lights on my shoulders;
no sighs but of my breathing; no tears but of
my shedding.   104

Tub. Yes, other men have ill luck too.   Antonio, as I heard in Genoa,—

Shy. What, what, what? ill luck, ill luck?

Tub. —hath an argosy cast away, coming 108
from Tripolis.

Shy. I thank God! I thank God! Is it true?
is it true?

Tub. I spoke with some of the sailors that 112
escaped the wrack.

Shy. I thank thee, good Tubal. Good news,
good news! ha, ha! Where? in Genoa?

Tub. Your daughter spent in Genoa, as I 116
heard, one night, fourscore ducats.

Shy. Thou stick'st a dagger in me: I shall
never see my gold again: fourscore ducats at a
sitting! fourscore ducats!   120

Tub. There came divers of Antonıo s creditors
in my company to Venice, that swear he cannot
choose but break.

Shy. I am very glad of it: I'll plague him; 124
I'll torture him: I am glad of it.

Tub. One of them showed me a ring that he
had of your daughter for a monkey.

Shy. Out upon her!   Thou torturest me, 128
Tubal: it was my turquoise; I had it of Leah
when I was a bachelor: I would not have given
it for a wilderness of monkeys.

Tub. But Antonio is certainly undone.   132

Shy. Nay, that's true, that's very true. Go,
Tubal, fee me an officer; bespeak him a fortnight

115 Where? in Genoa?; *cf. n.*
134 fee . . . officer: *engage a sheriff's officer for me*

before.   I will have the heart of him, if he forfeit; for, were he out of Venice, I can make what 136
merchandise I will.   Go, go, Tubal, and meet me
at our synagogue; go, good Tubal; at our synagogue, Tubal.   *Exeunt.*

Scene Two

[Belmont.   A Room in Portia's House]

*Enter Bassanio, Portia, Gratiano, [Nerissa,] and all
their Train.*

Por. I pray you, tarry: pause a day or two
Before you hazard; for, in choosing wrong,
I lose your company: therefore, forbear awhile.
There's something tells me, but it is not love,   4
I would not lose you; and you know yourself,
Hate counsels not in such a quality.
But lest you should not understand me well,—
And yet a maiden hath no tongue but thought,—   8
I would detain you here some month or two
Before you venture for me.   I could teach you
How to choose right, but then I am forsworn;
So will I never be: so may you miss me;   12
But if you do, you'll make me wish a sin,
That I had been forsworn.   Beshrew your eyes,
They have o'erlook'd me and divided me:
One half of me is yours, the other half yours,   16
Mine own, I would say; but if mine, then yours,
And so all yours.   O! these naughty times
Put bars between the owners and their rights;
And so, though yours, not yours.   Prove it so,   20

137 merchandise: *business*   6 *Hate prompts no such advice*
15 o'erlook'd: *looked over, i.e., bewitched*
20, 21 Prove it so, etc.; *cf. n.*

Let fortune go to hell for it, not I.
I speak too long; but 'tis to peise the time,
To eke it and to draw it out in length,
To stay you from election.

    Bass.   Let me choose;   24
For as I am, I live upon the rack.

    Por. Upon the rack, Bassanio! then confess
What treason there is mingled with your love.

    Bass. None but that ugly treason of mistrust,   28
Which makes me fear th' enjoying of my love:
There may as well be amity and life
'Tween snow and fire, as treason and my love.

    Por. Ay, but I fear you speak upon the rack,   32
Where men enforced do speak anything.

    Bass. Promise me life, and I'll confess the truth.

    Por. Well then, confess, and live.

    Bass.   'Confess' and 'love'
Had been the very sum of my confession: 36
O happy torment, when my torturer
Doth teach me answers for deliverance!
But let me to my fortune and the caskets.

    Por. Away then! I am lock'd in one of them: 40
If you do love me, you will find me out.
Nerissa and the rest, stand all aloof.
Let music sound while he doth make his choice;
Then, if he lose, he makes a swan-like end,   44
Fading in music: that the comparison
May stand more proper, my eye shall be the stream
And watery death-bed for him. He may win;
And what is music then? then music is   48
Even as the flourish when true subjects bow
To a new-crowned monarch: such it is

22 peise: *weigh down, retard*   23 eke: *add to*
28 mistrust: *doubt, uncertainty*   29 fear: *feel apprehensive about*
30 amity and life: *affectionate intercourse*
49 flourish: *trumbets at coronations*

As are those dulcet sounds in break of day
That creep into the dreaming bridegroom's ear,   52
And summon him to marriage.   Now he goes,
With no less presence, but with much more love,
Than young Alcides, when he did redeem
The virgin tribute paid by howling Troy   56
To the sea-monster: I stand for sacrifice;
The rest aloof are the Dardanian wives,
With bleared visages, come forth to view
The issue of the exploit.   Go, Hercules!   60
Live thou, I live: with much, much more dismay
I view the fight than thou that mak'st the fray.
Here Music.   A Song the whilst Bassanio comments on
the caskets to himself.

> 'Tell me where is fancy bred,
>   Or in the heart or in the head?   64
> How begot, how nourished?
>   Reply, reply.
> It is engender'd in the eyes,
> With gazing fed; and fancy dies   68
> In the cradle where it lies.
>   Let us all ring fancy's knell:
>   I'll begin it,—Ding, dong, bell.
> *All.* Ding, dong, bell.   72

Bass. So may the outward shows be least them-
   selves:
The world is still deceiv'd with ornament.
In law, what plea so tainted and corrupt
But, being season'd with a gracious voice,   76
Obscures the show of evil?   In religion,
What damned error, but some sober brow
Will bless it and approve it with a text,

54, 55 With . . . Alcides; *cf. n.*   54 presence: *dignity of person*
58 Dardanian: *Trojan*   63 fancy: *love*   79 approve: *prove, ratify*

Hiding the grossness with fair ornament?   80
There is no vice so simple but assumes
Some mark of virtue on his outward parts.
How many cowards, whose hearts are all as false
As stairs of sand, wear yet upon their chins   84
The beards of Hercules and frowning Mars,
Who, inward search'd, have livers white as milk;
And these assume but valour's excrement
To render them redoubted!   Look on beauty,   88
And you shall see 'tis purchas'd by the weight;
Which therein works a miracle in nature,
Making them lightest that wear most of it:
So are those crisped snaky golden locks   92
Which make such wanton gambols with the wind,
Upon supposed fairness, often known
To be the dowry of a second head,
The skull that bred them in the sepulchre.   96
Thus ornament is but the guiled shore
To a most dangerous sea; the beauteous scarf
Veiling an Indian beauty; in a word,
The seeming truth which cunning times put on   100
To entrap the wisest.   Therefore, thou gaudy gold,
Hard food for Midas, I will none of thee;
Nor none of thee, thou pale and common drudge
'Tween man and man: but thou, thou meagre lead,   104
Which rather threat'nest than dost promise aught,
Thy plainness moves me more than eloquence,
And here choose I: joy be the consequence!

    Por. [*Aside.*] How all the other passions fleet to air,
As doubtful thoughts, and rash-embrac'd despair,   109

---

81 simple: *pure, unmixed*   82 his: *its*
87 excrement: *excrescence*   91 lightest: *i.e., most frivolous*
92 crisped: *curled*   94 Upon supposed fairness; *cf. n.*
97 guiled: *guileful*   99 Veiling, etc.; *cf. n.*
102 Midas: *all he touched, including food, turned to gold*
109 As: *such as*

And shuddering fear, and green-ey'd jealousy.
O love! be moderate; allay thy ecstasy;
In measure rain thy joy; scant this excess;   112
I feel too much thy blessing; make it less,
For fear I surfeit!
 Bass.   What find I here?
         [Opening the leaden casket.]
Fair Portia's counterfeit! What demi-god
Hath come so near creation? Move these eyes?   116
Or whether, riding on the balls of mine,
Seem they in motion? Here are sever'd lips,
Parted with sugar breath; so sweet a bar
Should sunder such sweet friends. Here, in her hairs
The painter plays the spider, and hath woven   121
A golden mesh to entrap the hearts of men
Faster than gnats in cobwebs: but her eyes!—
How could he see to do them? having made one,   124
Methinks it should have power to steal both his
And leave itself unfurnish'd: yet look, how far
The substance of my praise doth wrong this shadow
In underprizing it, so far this shadow   128
Doth limp behind the substance. Here's the scroll,
The continent and summary of my fortune.

  'You that choose not by the view,
   Chance as fair and choose as true!   132
   Since this fortune falls to you,
   Be content and seek no new.
   If you be well pleas'd with this
   And hold your fortune for your bliss,   136
   Turn you where your lady is
   And claim her with a loving kiss.'

112 rain; *cf. n.*
126 unfurnish'd: *unaccompanied by its mate*
130 continent: *that which contains*

A gentle scroll.   Fair lady, by your leave;

                             [Kissing her.]

I come by note, to give and to receive.   140
Like one of two contending in a prize,
That thinks he hath done well in people's eyes,
Hearing applause and universal shout,
Giddy in spirit, still gazing in a doubt   144
Whether those peals of praise be his or no;
So, thrice-fair lady, stand I, even so,
As doubtful whether what I see be true,
Until confirm'd, sign'd, ratified by you.   148
   Por. You see me, Lord Bassanio, where I stand,
Such as I am: though for myself alone
I would not be ambitious in my wish,
To wish myself much better; yet for you   152
I would be trebled twenty times myself;
A thousand times more fair, ten thousand times
More rich;
That only to stand high in your account,   156
I might in virtues, beauties, livings, friends,
Exceed account: but the full sum of me
Is sum of nothing; which, to term in gross,
Is an unlesson'd girl, unschool'd, unpractis'd;   160
Happy in this, she is not yet so old
But she may learn; happier than this,
She is not bred so dull but she can learn;
Happiest of all is that her gentle spirit   164
Commits itself to yours to be directed,
As from her lord, her governor, her king.
Myself and what is mine to you and yours
Is now converted: but now I was the lord   168
Of this fair mansion, master of my servants,
Queen o'er myself; and even now, but now,

---

140 note: *authorization in writing*   158 account: *calculation*
159 term in gross: *sum up*   161 Happy: *fortunate*

This house, these servants, and this same myself
Are yours, my lord.   I give them with this ring;   172
Which when you part from, lose, or give away,
Let it presage the ruin of your love,
And be my vantage to exclaim on you.

Bass. Madam, you have bereft me of all words,   176
Only my blood speaks to you in my veins;
And there is such confusion in my powers,
As, after some oration fairly spoke
By a beloved prince, there doth appear   180
Among the buzzing pleased multitude;
Where every something, being blent together,
Turns to a wild of nothing, save of joy,
Express'd and not express'd.   But when this ring   184
Parts from this finger, then parts life from hence:
O! then be bold to say Bassanio's dead.

Ner. My lord and lady, it is now our time,
That have stood by and seen our wishes prosper,   188
To cry, good joy.   Good joy, my lord and lady!

Gra. My Lord Bassanio and my gentle lady,
I wish you all the joy that you can wish;
For I am sure you can wish none from me: 192
And when your honours mean to solemnize
The bargain of your faith, I do beseech you,
Even at that time I may be married too.

Bass. With all my heart, so thou canst get a wife.

Gra. I thank your lordship, you have got me one. 197
My eyes, my lord, can look as swift as yours:
You saw the mistress, I beheld the maid;
You lov'd, I lov'd; for intermission   200
No more pertains to me, my lord, than you.
Your fortune stood upon the caskets there,

175 vantage: *opportunity, occasion*
177 Only: *an adjective, my blood only*
192 from me: *at my expense*   200 intermission; *cf. n.*

And so did mine too, as the matter falls;
For wooing here until I sweat again,   204
And swearing till my very roof was dry
With oaths of love, at last, if promise last,
I got a promise of this fair one here
To have her love, provided that your fortune   208
Achiev'd her mistress.

    Por.   Is this true, Nerissa?

    Ner. Madam, it is, so you stand pleas'd withal.

    Bass. And do you, Gratiano, mean good faith?

    Gra. Yes, faith, my lord.   212

    Bass. Our feast shall be much honour'd in your marriage.

    Gra. We'll play with them the first boy for a
thousand ducats.

    Ner. What! and stake down?   216

    Gra. No; we shall ne'er win at that sport, and
stake down.

But who comes here? Lorenzo and his infidel?
What! and my old Venetian friend, Salanio?   220

    Enter Lorenzo, Jessica, and Salanio.

    Bass. Lorenzo, and Salanio, welcome hither,
If that the youth of my new interest here
Have power to bid you welcome. By your leave,
I bid my very friends and countrymen,   224
Sweet Portia, welcome.

    Por.   So do I, my lord:
They are entirely welcome.

    Lor. I thank your honour. For my part, my lord,
My purpose was not to have seen you here;   228
But meeting with Salanio by the way,
He did entreat me, past all saying nay,

204 until . . . again: *with all my power*
205 roof: *roof of my mouth*   220 Salanio; *cf. n.*   224 very: *true*

To come with him along.

   Salan.   I did, my lord,

And I have reason for it. Signior Antonio   232

Commends him to you.   [*Gives Bassanio a letter.*]

   Bass.   Ere I ope his letter,

I pray you, tell me how my good friend doth.

   Salan. Not sick, my lord, unless it be in mind;

Nor well, unless in mind: his letter there   234

Will show you his estate.

                   [*Bassanio*] *Opens the Letter.*

   Gra. Nerissa, cheer yon stranger; bid her welcome.

Your hand, Salanio. What's the news from Venice?

How doth that royal merchant, good Antonio?   240

I know he will be glad of our success;

We are the Jasons, we have won the fleece.

   Salan. I would you had won the fleece that he hath
      lost.

   Por. There are some shrewd contents in yon same
      paper,   244

That steals the colour from Bassanio's cheek:

Some dear friend dead, else nothing in the world

Could turn so much the constitution

Of any constant man. What, worse and worse!   248

With leave, Bassanio; I am half yourself,

And I must freely have the half of anything

That this same paper brings you.

   Bass.   O sweet Portia!

Here are a few of the unpleasant'st words   252

That ever blotted paper. Gentle lady,

When I did first impart my love to you,

I freely told you all the wealth I had

Ran in my veins, I was a gentleman: 256

And then I told you true; and yet, dear lady,

---

237 estate: *state, condition*   244 shrewd: *evil*

247 constitution: *frame of mind, equanimity*   248 constant: *steadfast*

Rating myself at nothing, you shall see
How much I was a braggart. When I told you
My state was nothing, I should then have told you   260
That I was worse than nothing; for, indeed,
I have engag'd myself to a dear friend,
Engag'd my friend to his mere enemy,
To feed my means. Here is a letter, lady;   264
The paper as the body of my friend,
And every word in it a gaping wound,
Issuing life-blood. But is it true, Salanio?
Hath all his ventures fail'd? What, not one hit?   268
From Tripolis, from Mexico, and England,
From Lisbon, Barbary, and India?
And not one vessel 'scape the dreadful touch
Of merchant-marring rocks?
   Salan.   Not one, my lord. 272
Besides, it should appear, that if he had
The present money to discharge the Jew,
He would not take it. Never did I know
A creature, that did bear the shape of man,   276
So keen and greedy to confound a man.
He plies the duke at morning and at night,
And doth impeach the freedom of the state,
If they deny him justice: twenty merchants,   280
The duke himself, and the magnificoes
Of greatest port, have all persuaded with him;
But none can drive him from the envious plea
Of forfeiture, of justice, and his bond.   284
   Jes. When I was with him, I have heard him swear
To Tubal and to Chus, his countrymen,
That he would rather have Antonio's flesh
Than twenty times the value of the sum   288

263 mere: *absolute*   268 hit: *successful venture*
277 confound: *destroy*   279 freedom: *equal rights*
281 magnificoes: *magnates*   282 port: *station*   283 envious: *hateful*

That he did owe him; and I know, my lord,
If law, authority, and power deny not,
It will go hard with poor Antonio.

  Por. Is it your dear friend that is thus in trouble?

  Bass. The dearest friend to me, the kindest man, 293
The best-condition'd and unwearied spirit
In doing courtesies, and one in whom
The ancient Roman honour more appears   296
Than any that draws breath in Italy.

  Por. What sum owes he the Jew?

  Bass. For me, three thousand ducats.

  Por.   What, no more?
Pay him six thousand, and deface the bond;   300
Double six thousand, and then treble that,
Before a friend of this description
Shall lose a hair thorough Bassanio's fault.
First go with me to church and call me wife,   304
And then away to Venice to your friend;
For never shall you lie by Portia's side
With an unquiet soul. You shall have gold
To pay the petty debt twenty times over: 308
When it is paid, bring your true friend along.
My maid Nerissa and myself meantime,
Will live as maids and widows. Come, away!
For you shall hence upon your wedding-day.   312
Bid your friends welcome, show a merry cheer;
Since you are dear bought, I will love you dear.
But let me hear the letter of your friend.

  Bass. 'Sweet Bassanio, my ships have all mis- 316
carried, my creditors grow cruel, my estate is very
low, my bond to the Jew is forfeit; and since, in
paying it, it is impossible I should live, all debts
are cleared between you and I, if I might but see 320

294 unwearied: *most unwearied*   300 deface: *cancel by writing across*
303 thorough: *through*   313 cheer: *face*

you at my death.   Notwithstanding, use your
pleasure: if your love do not persuade you to come,
let not my letter.'
Por. O love, dispatch all business, and be gone! 324
Bass. Since I have your good leave to go away,
   I will make haste; but, till I come again,
No bed shall e'er be guilty of my stay,
   Nor rest be interposer 'twixt us twain.   *Exeunt.*

Scene Three

[*Venice.   A Street*]

*Enter the Jew, and Salarino, and Antonio, and the
Gaoler.*

Shy. Gaoler, look to him: tell not me of mercy;
This is the fool that lent out money gratis:
Gaoler, look to him.
   Ant.   Hear me yet, good Shylock.
   Shy. I'll have my bond; speak not against my bond:
I have sworn an oath that I will have my bond.   5
Thou call'dst me dog before thou hadst a cause,
But, since I am a dog, beware my fangs:
The duke shall grant me justice.   I do wonder,   8
Thou naughty gaoler, that thou art so fond
To come abroad with him at his request.
   Ant. I pray thee, hear me speak.
   Shy. I'll have my bond; I will not hear thee speak:
I'll have my bond, and therefore speak no more.   13
I'll not be made a soft and dull-eyed fool,
To shake the head, relent, and sigh, and yield
To Christian intercessors.   Follow not;   16

1 Gaoler: *jailor*   9 naughty: *good-for-naught*

I'll have no speaking; I will have my bond.

Exit Jew.

    Salar. It is the most impenetrable cur
That ever kept with men.
    Ant.   Let him alone:
I'll follow him no more with bootless prayers.   20
He seeks my life; his reason well I know.
I oft deliver'd from his forfeitures
Many that have at times made moan to me;
Therefore he hates me.
    Salar.   I am sure the duke   24
Will never grant this forfeiture to hold.
    Ant. The duke cannot deny the course of law:
For the commodity that strangers have
With us in Venice, if it be denied,   28
'Twill much impeach the justice of the state;
Since that the trade and profit of the city
Consisteth of all nations. Therefore, go:
These griefs and losses have so bated me,   32
That I shall hardly spare a pound of flesh
To-morrow to my bloody creditor.
Well, gaoler, on. Pray God, Bassanio come
To see me pay his debt, and then I care not!   36

Exeunt.

Scene Four

[Belmont. A Room in Portia's House]

*Enter Portia, Nerissa, Lorenzo, Jessica, and a man of
Portia's [Balthazar].*

    Lor. Madam, although I speak it in your presence,
You have a noble and a true conceit

19 kept: *dwelt*   26 deny: *refuse*
27 commodity: *trading facilities*   30 trade and profit: *profitable trade*
32 bated: *thinned*   2 conceit: *conception*

Of godlike amity; which appears most strongly
In bearing thus the absence of your lord.   4
But if you knew to whom you show this honour,
How true a gentleman you send relief,
How dear a lover of my lord your husband,
I know you would be prouder of the work   8
Than customary bounty can enforce you.

   Por. I never did repent for doing good,
Nor shall not now: for in companions
That do converse and waste the time together,   12
Whose souls do bear an equal yoke of love,
There must be needs a like proportion
Of lineaments, of manners, and of spirit;
Which makes me think that this Antonio,   16
Being the bosom lover of my lord,
Must needs be like my lord. If it be so,
How little is the cost I have bestow'd
In purchasing the semblance of my soul   20
From out the state of hellish cruelty!
This comes too near the praising of myself;
Therefore, no more of it: hear other things.
Lorenzo, I commit into your hands   24
The husbandry and manage of my house
Until my lord's return: for mine own part,
I have toward heaven breath'd a secret vow
To live in prayer and contemplation,   28
Only attended by Nerissa here,
Until her husband and my lord's return.
There is a monastery two miles off,
And there will we abide. I do desire you   32
Not to deny this imposition,
The which my love and some necessity

9 customary bounty: *ordinary benevolence*   enforce: *cause to be*
20 semblance . . . soul; *cf. n.*
25 husbandry and manage: *care and management*
33 deny this imposition: *decline this charge*

Now lays upon you.

  Lor.   Madam, with all my heart:

I shall obey you in all fair commands.   **36**

  Por. My people do already know my mind,

And will acknowledge you and Jessica

In place of Lord Bassanio and myself.

So fare you well till we shall meet again.   40

  Lor. Fair thoughts and happy hours attend on you!

  Jes. I wish your ladyship all heart's content.

  Por. I thank you for your wish, and am well pleas'd

To wish it back on you: fare you well, Jessica.   44

       Exeunt [*Jessica and Lorenzo*].

Now, Balthazar,

As I have ever found thee honest-true,

So let me find thee still. Take this same letter,

And use thou all the endeavour of a man   **48**

In speed to Padua: see thou render this

Into my cousin's hand, Doctor Bellario;

And, look, what notes and garments he doth give thee,

Bring them, I pray thee, with imagin'd speed   **52**

Unto the tranect, to the common ferry

Which trades to Venice. Waste no time in words,

But get thee gone: I shall be there before thee.

  Balth. Madam, I go with all convenient speed. **56**

          [*Exit.*]

  Por. Come on, Nerissa: I have work in hand

That you yet know not of: we'll see our husbands

Before they think of us.

  Ner.   Shall they see us?

  Por. They shall, Nerissa; but in such a habit   60

That they shall think we are accomplished

With that we lack. I'll hold thee any wager,

---

50 cousin's: *any collateral kin*   52 imagin'd speed: *speed of thought*
53 tranect; *cf. n.*   56 convenient: *becoming*
61 accomplished: *equipped*

When we are both accoutred like young men,
I'll prove the prettier fellow of the two,   64
And wear my dagger with the braver grace,
And speak between the change of man and boy
With a reed voice, and turn two mincing steps
Into a manly stride, and speak of frays   68
Like a fine bragging youth, and tell quaint lies,
How honourable ladies sought my love,
Which I denying, they fell sick and died:
I could not do withal; then I'll repent,   72
And wish, for all that, that I had not kill'd them:
And twenty of these puny lies I'll tell,
That men shall swear I have discontinu'd school
Above a twelvemonth. I have within my mind   76
A thousand raw tricks of these bragging Jacks,
Which I will practise.
    Ner.   Why, shall we turn to men?
    Por.   Fie, what a question's that,
If thou wert near a lewd interpreter!   80
But come: I'll tell thee all my whole device
When I am in my coach, which stays for us
At the park gate; and therefore haste away,
For we must measure twenty miles to-day.   84
                                Exeunt.

Scene Five

[*The Same. A Garden*]

Enter Clown and Jessica.

    Laun. Yes, truly; for, look you, the sins of
the father are to be laid upon the children; therefore, I promise you, I fear you. I was always
plain with you, and so now I speak my agitation 4

---

72 could not do withal: *could not help it*   3 fear: *fear for*
4 agitation: *i.e., cogitation*

of the matter: therefore be of good cheer; for, truly, I think you are damned. There is but one hope in it that can do you any good, and that is but a kind of bastard hope neither.   8

Jes. And what hope is that, I pray thee?

Laun. Marry, you may partly hope that your father got you not, that you are not the Jew's daughter.   12

Jes. That were a kind of bastard hope, indeed: so the sins of my mother should be visited upon me.

Laun. Truly then I fear you are damned both 16 by father and mother: thus when I shun Scylla, your father, I fall into Charybdis, your mother: well, you are gone both ways.

Jes. I shall be saved by my husband; he hath 20 made me a Christian.

Laun. Truly the more to blame he: we were Christians enow before; e'en as many as could well live one by another. This making of Chris- 24 tians will raise the price of hogs: if we grow all to be pork-eaters, we shall not shortly have a rasher on the coals for money.

Jes. I'll tell my husband, Launcelot, what you 28 say: here he comes.

Enter Lorenzo.

Lor. I shall grow jealous of you shortly, Launcelot, if you thus get my wife into corners.   32

Jes. Nay, you need not fear us, Lorenzo: Launcelot and I are out. He tells me flatly,

---

8 neither: *too*
17, 18 Scylla . . . Charybdis: *dangers confronting Ulysses*
20 husband; *cf. n.*

there is no mercy for me in heaven, because I
am a Jew's daughter: and he says you are no 36
good member of the commonwealth, for, in con-
verting Jews to Christians, you raise the price of
pork.

Lor. I shall answer that better to the com- 40
monwealth than you can the getting up of the
negro's belly: the Moor is with child by you,
Launcelot.

Laun. It is much that the Moor should be 44
more than reason; but if she be less than an
honest woman, she is indeed more than I took
her for.

Lor. How every fool can play upon the word! 48
I think the best grace of wit will shortly turn
into silence, and discourse grow commendable
in none only but parrots. Go in, sirrah: bid
them prepare for dinner.   52

Laun. That is done, sir; they have all
stomachs.

Lor. Goodly Lord, what a wit-snapper are
you! then bid them prepare dinner.   56

Laun. That is done too, sir; only, 'cover' is
the word.

Lor. Will you cover, then, sir?

Laun. Not so, sir, neither; I know my duty.   60

Lor. Yet more quarrelling with occasion!
Wilt thou show the whole wealth of thy wit in
an instant? I pray thee, understand a plain man
in his plain meaning: go to thy fellows; bid 64
them cover the table, serve in the meat, and we
will come in to dinner.

Laun. For the table, sir, it shall be served in;

for the meat, sir, it shall be covered; for your 68
coming in to dinner, sir, why, let it be as humours and conceits shall govern.   *Exit Clown.*

Lor. O dear discretion, how his words are suited!
The fool hath planted in his memory   72
An army of good words: and I do know
A many fools, that stand in better place,
Garnish'd like him, that for a tricksy word
Defy the matter. How cheer'st thou, Jessica?   76
And now, good sweet, say thy opinion;
How dost thou like the Lord Bassanio's wife?

Jes. Past all expressing. It is very meet,
The Lord Bassanio live an upright life,   80
For, having such a blessing in his lady,
He finds the joys of heaven here on earth;
And if on earth he do not mean it, then
In reason he should never come to heaven.   84
Why, if two gods should play some heavenly match,
And on the wager lay two earthly women,
And Portia one, there must be something else
Pawn'd with the other, for the poor rude world   88
Hath not her fellow.

Lor.   Even such a husband
Hast thou of me as she is for a wife.

Jes. Nay, but ask my opinion too of that.

Lor. I will anon; first, let us go to dinner.   92

Jes. Nay, let me praise you while I have a stomach.

Lor. No, pray thee, let it serve for table-talk;
Then howsoe'er thou speak'st, 'mong other things
I shall digest it.

Jes.   Well, I'll set you forth.   *Exeunt.*

69 humours: *whims*   71 suited: *elaborately dressed*
76 Defy the matter: *spoil the thought*   How cheer'st thou: *what*
    cheer?   *cheer?*
83 mean it; *cf. n.*   88 Pawn'd: *staked*

ACT FOURTH

Scene One

[Venice. A Court of Justice]

Enter the Duke, the Magnificoes, Antonio, Bassanio,
and Gratiano [with Salarino, Salanio, and Others].

 Duke. What, is Antonio here?
 Ant. Ready, so please your Grace.
 Duke. I am sorry for thee: thou art come to answer
A stony adversary, an inhuman wretch   4
Uncapable of pity, void and empty
From any dram of mercy.
 Ant.   I have heard
Your Grace hath ta'en great pains to qualify
His rigorous course; but since he stands obdurate, 8
And that no lawful means can carry me
Out of his envy's reach, I do oppose
My patience to his fury, and am arm'd
To suffer with a quietness of spirit   12
The very tyranny and rage of his.
 Duke. Go one, and call the Jew into the court.
 Salar. He's ready at the door: he comes, my lord.

Enter Shylock.

 Duke. Make room, and let him stand before our
  face.   16
Shylock, the world thinks, and I think so too,
That thou but lead'st this fashion of thy malice
To the last hour of act; and then 'tis thought
Thou'lt show thy mercy and remorse more strange 20

3 answer: *satisfy*   6 dram: *drop*   7 qualify: *moderate*
13 tyranny and rage: *violent dominance*   18 fashion: *pretence*
19 act: *performance*   20 remorse: *pity*

Than is thy strange apparent cruelty;
And where thou now exact'st the penalty,—
Which is a pound of this poor merchant's flesh,—
Thou wilt not only loose the forfeiture,   24
But, touch'd with human gentleness and love,
Forgive a moiety of the principal;
Glancing an eye of pity on his losses,
That have of late so huddled on his back,   28
Enow to press a royal merchant down,
And pluck commiseration of his state
From brassy bosoms and rough hearts of flint,
From stubborn Turks and Tartars, never train'd   32
To offices of tender courtesy.
We all expect a gentle answer, Jew.

    Shy. I have possess'd your Grace of what I purpose;
And by our holy Sabbath have I sworn   36
To have the due and forfeit of my bond:
If you deny it, let the danger light
Upon your charter and your city's freedom.
You'll ask me why I rather choose to have   40
A weight of carrion flesh than to receive
Three thousand ducats: I'll not answer that:
But say it is my humour: is it answer'd?
What if my house be troubled with a rat,   44
And I be pleas'd to give ten thousand ducats
To have it ban'd? What, are you answer'd yet?
Some men there are love not a gaping pig;
Some, that are mad if they behold a cat;   48
And others, when the bagpipe sings i' the nose,
Cannot contain their urine: for affection
Masters our passion, sways it to the mood

---

24 loose: *release*   26 moiety: *portion (two syllables only)*
28 huddled: *crowded*   37 due and forfeit: *forfeit that is due*
38 danger: *damage*   46 ban'd: *poisoned*
47 gaping pig: *pig roasted with the mouth open*
50 affection: *natural bent of mind*

Of what it likes, or loathes.   Now, for your answer: 52
As there is no firm reason to be render'd,
Why he cannot abide a gaping pig;
Why he, a harmless necessary cat;
Why he, a woollen bagpipe; but of force   56
Must yield to such inevitable shame
As to offend, himself being offended;
So can I give no reason, nor I will not,
More than a lodg'd hate and a certain loathing   60
I bear Antonio, that I follow thus
A losing suit against him.   Are you answer'd?
     Bass. This is no answer, thou unfeeling man,
To excuse the current of thy cruelty.   64
     Shy. I am not bound to please thee with my answer.
     Bass. Do all men kill the things they do not love?
     Shy. Hates any man the thing he would not kill?
     Bass. Every offence is not a hate at first. 68
     Shy. What! wouldst thou have a serpent sting thee
          twice?
     Ant. I pray you, think you question with the Jew:
You may as well go stand upon the beach,
And bid the main flood bate his usual height;   72
You may as well use question with the wolf,
Why he hath made the ewe bleat for the lamb;
You may as well forbid the mountain pines
To wag their high tops, and to make no noise   76
When they are fretted with the gusts of heaven;
You may as well do anything most hard,
As seek to soften that—than which what's harder?—
His Jewish heart: therefore, I do beseech you,   80
Make no more offers, use no further means;

56 woollen; *cf. n.*
64 current: *steady flow*
70 question: *converse*
73, 74 *Cf. n.*

62 losing: *moneyless, unprofitable*
68 offence: *resentment*
72 bate: *reduce*
76 and: *and bid them*

But with all brief and plain conveniency,
Let me have judgment, and the Jew his will.

   Bass. For thy three thousand ducats here is six. 84

   Shy. If every ducat in six thousand ducats
Were in six parts and every part a ducat,
I would not draw them; I would have my bond.

   Duke. How shalt thou hope for mercy, rendering
     none? 88

   Shy. What judgment shall I dread, doing no wrong?
You have among you many a purchas'd slave,
Which, like your asses and your dogs and mules,
You use in abject and in slavish parts, 92
Because you bought them: shall I say to you,
Let them be free, marry them to your heirs?
Why sweat they under burdens? let their beds
Be made as soft as yours, and let their palates 96
Be season'd with such viands? You will answer:
'The slaves are ours:' so do I answer you:
The pound of flesh which I demand of him,
Is dearly bought; 'tis mine and I will have it. 100
If you deny me, fie upon your law!
There is no force in the decrees of Venice.
I stand for judgment: answer; shall I have it?

   Duke. Upon my power I may dismiss this court, 104
Unless Bellario, a learned doctor,
Whom I have sent for to determine this,
Come here to-day.

   Salar.   My lord, here stays without
A messenger with letters from the doctor, 108
New come from Padua.

   Duke. Bring us the letters: call the messenger.

   Bass. Good cheer, Antonio! What, man, courage
     yet!

87 draw: *receive*   92 parts: *actions*   97 season'd: *gratified*
104 Upon . . . power: *by authority vested in me*

The Jew shall have my flesh, blood, bones, and all, 112
Ere thou shalt lose for me one drop of blood.

Ant. I am a tainted wether of the flock,
Meetest for death: the weakest kind of fruit
Drops earliest to the ground; and so let me: 116
You cannot better be employ'd, Bassanio,
Than to live still, and write mine epitaph.

Enter Nerissa [dressed like a lawyer's clerk].

Duke. Came you from Padua, from Bellario?
Ner. From both, my lord. Bellario greets your
    Grace. [*Presents a letter.*] 120
Bass. Why dost thou whet thy knife so earnestly?
Shy. To cut the forfeiture from that bankrupt there.
Gra. Not on thy sole, but on thy soul, harsh Jew,
Thou mak'st thy knife keen; but no metal can, 124
No, not the hangman's axe, bear half the keenness
Of thy sharp envy. Can no prayers pierce thee?
Shy. No, none that thou hast wit enough to make.
Gra. O, be thou damn'd, inexecrable dog! 128
And for thy life let justice be accus'd.
Thou almost mak'st me waver in my faith
To hold opinion with Pythagoras,
That souls of animals infuse themselves 132
Into the trunks of men: thy currish spirit
Govern'd a wolf, who, hang'd for human slaughter,
Even from the gallows did his fell soul fleet,
And whilst thou lay'st in thy unhallow'd dam, 136
Infus'd itself in thee; for thy desires
Are wolfish, bloody, starv'd, and ravenous.
Shy. Till thou canst rail the seal from off my bond,
Thou but offend'st thy lungs to speak so loud: 140

118 *Cf. n.*
128 inexecrable: *who cannot be execrated enough*
129 justice; *cf. n.*

Repair thy wit, good youth, or it will fall
To cureless ruin. I stand here for law.

Duke. This letter from Bellario doth commend
A young and learned doctor to our court.   144
Where is he?

Ner.   He attendeth here hard by,
To know your answer, whether you'll admit him.

Duke. With all my heart: some three or four of you
Go give him courteous conduct to this place.   148
Meantime, the court shall hear Bellario's letter.

[*Clerk*]. 'Your Grace shall understand that at the
receipt of your letter I am very sick; but in the
instant that your messenger came, in loving visi- 152
tation was with me a young doctor of Rome; his
name is Balthazar. I acquainted him with the
cause in controversy between the Jew and Antonio
the merchant: we turned o'er many books toge- 156
ther: he is furnished with my opinion; which,
bettered with his own learning,—the greatness
whereof I cannot enough commend,—comes with
him, at my importunity, to fill up your Grace's 160
request in my stead. I beseech you, let his lack
of years be no impediment to let him lack a reverend estimation, for I never knew so young a
body with so old a head. I leave him to your 164
gracious acceptance, whose trial shall better publish his commendation.'

Duke. You hear the learn'd Bellario, what he
writes:
And here, I take it, is the doctor come.   168

142 cureless: *incurable*   148 conduct: *escort*
149 letter; *cf. n.*   162 reverend estimation: *respectful esteem*
165, 166 publish . . . commendation: *make known his merit*

*Enter Portia for Balthazar [dressed like a doctor of
laws].*

Give me your hand.   Came you from old Bellario?

   Por. I did, my lord.

   Duke.   You are welcome: take your place.

Are you acquainted with the difference

That holds this present question in the court?   172

   Por. I am informed throughly of the cause.

Which is the merchant here, and which the Jew?

   Duke. Antonio and old Shylock, both stand forth.

   Por. Is your name Shylock?

   Shy.   Shylock is my name. 176

   Por. Of a strange nature is the suit you follow;

Yet in such rule that the Venetian law

Cannot impugn you as you do proceed.

[*To Antonio.*] You stand within his danger, do you

      not?   180

   Ant. Ay, so he says.

   Por.   Do you confess the bond?

   Ant. I do.

   Por.   Then must the Jew be merciful.

   Shy. On what compulsion must I? tell me that.

   Por. The quality of mercy is not strain'd,   184

It droppeth as the gentle rain from heaven

Upon the place beneath: it is twice bless'd;

It blesseth him that gives and him that takes:

'Tis mightiest in the mightiest; it becomes   188

The throned monarch better than his crown;

His sceptre shows the force of temporal power,

The attribute to awe and majesty,

Wherein doth sit the dread and fear of kings;   192

---

171 difference: *dispute*   173 throughly: *thoroughly*
178 rule: *correct mode of procedure*   179 impugn: *oppose*
180 danger: *power to hurt*   184 strain'd: *constrained, forced*
191 The attribute: *what belongs*   awe and majesty: *awful majesty*

But mercy is above this sceptred sway,
It is enthroned in the hearts of kings,
It is an attribute to God himself,
And earthly power doth then show likest God's   196
When mercy seasons justice.   Therefore, Jew,
Though justice be thy plea, consider this,
That in the course of justice none of us
Should see salvation: we do pray for mercy,   200
And that same prayer doth teach us all to render
The deeds of mercy.   I have spoke thus much
To mitigate the justice of thy plea,
Which if thou follow, this strict court of Venice   204
Must needs give sentence 'gainst the merchant there.

Shy. My deeds upon my head!   I crave the law,
The penalty and forfeit of my bond.

Por. Is he not able to discharge the money?   208

Bass. Yes, here I tender it for him in the court;
Yea, twice the sum: if that will not suffice,
I will be bound to pay it ten times o'er,
On forfeit of my hands, my head, my heart.   212
If this will not suffice, it must appear
That malice bears down truth.   And, I beseech you,
Wrest once the law to your authority:
To do a great right, do a little wrong,   216
And curb this cruel devil of his will.

Por. It must not be.   There is no power in Venice
Can alter a decree established:
'Twill be recorded for a precedent,   220
And many an error by the same example
Will rush into the state.   It cannot be.

Shy. A Daniel come to judgment! yea, a Daniel!
O wise young judge, how I do honour thee!   224

197 seasons: *flavors*   214 truth: *equity*
215 Wrest: *strain*   to: *to the advantage of*
223 Daniel; *cf. n.*

Por. I pray you, let me look upon the bond.

Shy. Here 'tis, most reverend doctor; here it is.

Por. Shylock, there's thrice thy money offer'd thee.

Shy. An oath, an oath, I have an oath in heaven: 228
Shall I lay perjury upon my soul?
No, not for Venice.

Por.   Why, this bond is forfeit;
And lawfully by this the Jew may claim
A pound of flesh, to be by him cut off   232
Nearest the merchant's heart.   Be merciful:
Take thrice thy money; bid me tear the bond.

Shy. When it is paid according to the tenour.
It doth appear you are a worthy judge;   236
You know the law, your exposition
Hath been most sound: I charge you by the law,
Whereof you are a well-deserving pillar,
Proceed to judgment: by my soul I swear   240
There is no power in the tongue of man
To alter me.   I stay here on my bond.

Ant. Most heartily I do beseech the court
To give the judgment.

Por.   Why then, thus it is: 244
You must prepare your bosom for his knife.

Shy. O noble judge! O excellent young man!

Por. For the intent and purpose of the law
Hath full relation to the penalty,   248
Which here appeareth due upon the bond.

Shy. 'Tis very true!   O wise and upright judge!
How much more elder art thou than thy looks!

Por. Therefore lay bare your bosom.

Shy.   Ay, 'his breast:' 252
So says the bond:—doth it not, noble judge?—
'Nearest his heart:' those are the very words.

242 stay . . . on: *await the fulfilment of*

Por. It is so.   Are there balance here to weigh
The flesh?   256

Shy. I have them ready.

Por. Have by some surgeon, Shylock, on your
    charge,
To stop his wounds, lest he do bleed to death.

Shy. Is it so nominated in the bond?   260

Por. It is not so express'd; but what of that?
'Twere good you do so much for charity.

Shy. I cannot find it: 'tis not in the bond.

Por. You, merchant, have you anything to say? 264

Ant. But little: I am arm'd and well prepar'd.
Give me your hand, Bassanio: fare you well!
Grieve not that I am fallen to this for you;
For herein Fortune shows herself more kind   268
Than is her custom: it is still her use
To let the wretched man outlive his wealth,
To view with hollow eye and wrinkled brow
An age of poverty; from which lingering penance   272
Of such a misery doth she cut me off.
Commend me to your honourable wife:
Tell her the process of Antonio's end;
Say how I lov'd you, speak me fair in death;   276
And, when the tale is told, bid her be judge
Whether Bassanio had not once a love.
Repent but you that you shall lose your friend,
And he repents not that he pays your debt;   280
For if the Jew do cut but deep enough,
I'll pay it instantly with all my heart.

Bass. Antonio, I am married to a wife
Which is as dear to me as life itself;   284

255 balance: *scales*   258 on . . . charge: *at your expense*
269 use: *habit*   275 process: *story*
276 speak . . . fair: *speak well of me*   278 love: *devoted friend*
279 Repent: *repine, grieve*   284 Which: *who*

But life itself, my wife, and all the world,
Are not with me esteem'd above thy life:
I would lose all, ay, sacrifice them all,
Here to this devil, to deliver you.   288

   Por. Your wife would give you little thanks for that,
If she were by to hear you make the offer.

   Gra. I have a wife, whom, I protest, I love:
I would she were in heaven, so she could   292
Entreat some power to change this currish Jew.

   Ner. 'Tis well you offer it behind her back;
The wish would make else an unquiet house.

   Shy. These be the Christian husbands! I have a
     daughter;   296
Would any of the stock of Barabbas
Had been her husband rather than a Christian!
We trifle time; I pray thee, pursue sentence.

   Por. A pound of that same merchant's flesh is thine:
The court awards it, and the law doth give it.   301

   Shy. Most rightful judge!

   Por. And you must cut this flesh from off his breast:
The law allows it, and the court awards it.   304

   Shy. Most learned judge! A sentence! come, pre-
     pare!

   Por. Tarry a little: there is something else.
This bond doth give thee here no jot of blood;
The words expressly are 'a pound of flesh:'   308
Then take thy bond, take thou thy pound of flesh;
But, in the cutting it, if thou dost shed
One drop of Christian blood, thy lands and goods
Are, by the laws of Venice, confiscate   312
Unto the state of Venice.

   Gra. O upright judge! Mark, Jew: O learned judge!

   Shy. Is that the law?

299 pursue: *proceed with*

Por.   Thyself shalt see the act;
For, as thou urgest justice, be assur'd   316
Thou shalt have justice, more than thou desir'st.

   Gra. O learned judge! Mark, Jew: a learned judge!

   Shy. I take this offer then: pay the bond thrice,
And let the Christian go.

   Bass.   Here is the money.   320

   Por. Soft!
The Jew shall have all justice; soft! no haste:—
He shall have nothing but the penalty.

   Gra. O Jew! an upright judge, a learned judge!   324

   Por. Therefore prepare thee to cut off the flesh.
Shed thou no blood; nor cut thou less, nor more,
But just a pound of flesh: if thou tak'st more,
Or less, than a just pound, be it but so much   328
As makes it light or heavy in the substance,
Or the division of the twentieth part
Of one poor scruple, nay, if the scale do turn
But in the estimation of a hair,   332
Thou diest and all thy goods are confiscate.

   Gra. A second Daniel, a Daniel, Jew!
Now, infidel, I have thee on the hip.

   Por. Why doth the Jew pause? take thy forfeiture.

   Shy. Give me my principal, and let me go.   337

   Bass. I have it ready for thee; here it is.

   Por. He hath refus'd it in the open court:
He shall have merely justice, and his bond.   340

   Gra. A Daniel, still say I; a second Daniel!
I thank thee, Jew, for teaching me that word.

   Shy. Shall I not have barely my principal?

   Por. Thou shalt have nothing but the forfeiture, 344
To be so taken at thy peril, Jew.

---

328 just: *precise*   329 substance: *amount*
331 scruple: *one-third of a dram, twenty grains*
332 estimation: *calculation*

Shy. Why, then the devil give him good of it!
I'll stay no longer question.

    Por.   Tarry, Jew:
The law hath yet another hold on you.   348
It is enacted in the laws of Venice,
If it be prov'd against an alien
That by direct or indirect attempts
He seek the life of any citizen,   352
The party 'gainst the which he doth contrive
Shall seize one half his goods; the other half
Comes to the privy coffer of the state;
And the offender's life lies in the mercy   356
Of the duke only, 'gainst all other voice.
In which predicament, I say, thou stand'st;
For it appears by manifest proceeding,
That indirectly and directly too   360
Thou hast contriv'd against the very life
Of the defendant; and thou hast incurr'd
The danger formerly by me rehears'd.
Down therefore and beg mercy of the duke.   364

    Gra. Beg that thou mayst have leave to hang thy-
        self:
And yet, thy wealth being forfeit to the state,
Thou hast not left the value of a cord;
Therefore thou must be hang'd at the state's charge.

    Duke. That thou shalt see the difference of our
        spirits,   369
I pardon thee thy life before thou ask it.
For half thy wealth, it is Antonio's;
The other half comes to the general state,   372
Which humbleness may drive unto a fine.

    Por. Ay, for the state; not for Antonio.

---

353 contrive: *plot*   355 privy coffer: *treasury*
357 'gainst . . . voice: *in spite of what other persons may judge*
363 formerly: *above*   373 drive: *reduce*

Shy. Nay, take my life and all; pardon not that:
You take my house when you do take the prop   376
That doth sustain my house; you take my life
When you do take the means whereby I live.

Por. What mercy can you render him, Antonio? 379

Gra. A halter gratis; nothing else, for God's sake!

Ant. So please my lord the duke, and all the court,
To quit the fine for one half of his goods,
I am content; so he will let me have
The other half in use, to render it,   384
Upon his death, unto the gentleman
That lately stole his daughter:
Two things provided more, that, for this favour,
He presently become a Christian;   388
The other, that he do record a gift,
Here in the court, of all he dies possess'd,
Unto his son Lorenzo, and his daughter.

Duke. He shall do this, or else I do recant   392
The pardon that I late pronounced here.

Por. Art thou contented, Jew? what dost thou say?

Shy. I am content.

Por.   Clerk, draw a deed of gift.

Shy. I pray you give me leave to go from hence: 396
I am not well. Send the deed after me,
And I will sign it.

Duke.   Get thee gone, but do it.

Gra. In christening thou shalt have two godfathers;
Had I been judge, thou shouldst have had ten more,
To bring thee to the gallows, not the font.   401

                                Exit [*Shylock*].

Duke. Sir, I entreat you home with me to dinner.

Por. I humbly do desire your Grace of pardon:
I must away this night toward Padua,   404

390 of all: *of all of which*   400 ten more: *i.e., a jury of twelve*

And it is meet I presently set forth.

    Duke. I am sorry that your leisure serves you not.
Antonio, gratify this gentleman,
For, in my mind, you are much bound to him.   **408**

        Exit Duke [with Magnificoes] and his train.

    Bass. Most worthy gentleman, I and my friend
Have by your wisdom been this day acquitted
Of grievous penalties; in lieu whereof,
Three thousand ducats, due unto the Jew,   **412**
We freely cope your courteous pains withal.

    Ant. And stand indebted, over and above,
In love and service to you evermore.

    Por. He is well paid that is well satisfied;   **416**
And I, delivering you, am satisfied,
And therein do account myself well paid:
My mind was never yet more mercenary.
I pray you, know me when we meet again: **420**
I wish you well, and so I take my leave.

    Bass. Dear sir, of force I must attempt you further:
Take some remembrance of us, as a tribute,
Not as a fee. Grant me two things, I pray you,   **424**
Not to deny me, and to pardon me.

    Por. You press me far, and therefore I will yield.
[*To Antonio.*] Give me your gloves, I'll wear them for
      your sake;
[*To Bassanio.*] And, for your love, I'll take this ring
      from you.   **428**
Do not draw back your hand; I'll take no more;
And you in love shall not deny me this.

    Bass. This ring, good sir? alas! it is a trifle;
I will not shame myself to give you this.   **432**

    Por. I will have nothing else but only this;
And now methinks I have a mind to it.

407 gratify: *reward*   413 cope: *match, requite*
422 force: *necessity*   attempt: *tempt, urge*

Bass. There's more depends on this than on the
value.

The dearest ring in Venice will I give you,   436
And find it out by proclamation:
Only for this, I pray you, pardon me.

    Por. I see, sir, you are liberal in offers:
You taught me first to beg, and now methinks   440
You teach me how a beggar should be answer'd.

    Bass. Good sir, this ring was given me by my wife;
And when she put it on, she made me vow
That I should never sell nor give nor lose it.   444

    Por. That 'scuse serves many men to save their
gifts.
And if your wife be not a mad-woman,
And know how well I have deserv'd the ring,
She would not hold out enemy for ever,   448
For giving it to me. Well, peace be with you.

                    Exeunt [*Portia and Nerissa*].

    Ant. My Lord Bassanio, let him have the ring:
Let his deservings and my love withal
Be valu'd 'gainst your wife's commandment.   452

    Bass. Go, Gratiano; run and overtake him;
Give him the ring, and bring him, if thou canst,
Unto Antonio's house. Away! make haste.

                            Exit Gratiano.

Come, you and I will thither presently,   456
And in the morning early will we both
Fly toward Belmont. Come, Antonio.   *Exeunt.*

---

437 proclamation: *advertisement (through the street crier)*

Scene Two

[*The Same.   A Street*]

Enter Portia and Nerissa.

Por. Inquire the Jew's house out, give him this deed,
And let him sign it.   We'll away to-night,
And be a day before our husbands home:
This deed will be well welcome to Lorenzo.   4

Enter Gratiano.

Gra. Fair sir, you are well o'erta'en.
My Lord Bassanio upon more advice
Hath sent you here this ring, and doth entreat
Your company at dinner.
Por.   That cannot be: 8
His ring I do accept most thankfully;
And so, I pray you, tell him: furthermore,
I pray you, show my youth old Shylock's house.
Gra. That will I do.
Ner.   Sir, I would speak with you. 12
[*Aside to Portia.*] I'll see if I can get my husband's
    ring,
Which I did make him swear to keep for ever.
Por. Thou mayst, I warrant.   We shall have old
    swearing
That they did give the rings away to men;   16
But we'll outface them, and outswear them too.
Away ! make haste: thou know'st where I will tarry.
Ner. Come, good sir, will you show me to this house?
                                        Exeunt.

6 advice: *consideration*   15 old: *much*

ACT FIFTH

Scene One

[Belmont.   The Avenue to Portia's House]

Enter Lorenzo and Jessica.

Lor. The moon shines bright: in such a night as this,
When the sweet wind did gently kiss the trees
And they did make no noise, in such a night
Troilus methinks mounted the Troyan walls,   4
And sigh'd his soul toward the Grecian tents,
Where Cressid lay that night.

Jes.   In such a night
Did Thisbe fearfully o'ertrip the dew,
And saw the lion's shadow ere himself,   8
And ran dismay'd away.

Lor.   In such a night
Stood Dido with a willow in her hand
Upon the wild sea-banks, and waft her love
To come again to Carthage.

Jes.   In such a night   12
Medea gather'd the enchanted herbs
That did renew old Æson.

Lor.   In such a night
Did Jessica steal from the wealthy Jew,
And with an unthrift love did run from Venice,   16
As far as Belmont.

Jes.   In such a night
Did young Lorenzo swear he lov'd her well,
Stealing her soul with many vows of faith,

4 Troilus: *cf. Shakespeare's play on the theme*
7 Thisbe: *cf. Midsummer Night's Dream*
10 willow: *emblem of slighted love*   11 waft: *beckoned*
14 renew: *rejuvenate*   Æson: *father of Jason*

And ne'er a true one.

 Lor.   In such a night   20
Did pretty Jessica, like a little shrew,
Slander her love, and he forgave it her.

 Jes. I would out-night you, did nobody come;
But, hark! I hear the footing of a man.   24

Enter Messenger [*Stephano*].

 Lor. Who comes so fast in silence of the night?
 Mes. A friend.
 Lor. A friend! what friend? your name, I pray you,
  friend.
 Mes. Stephano is my name; and I bring word 28
My mistress will before the break of day
Be here at Belmont: she doth stray about
By holy crosses, where she kneels and prays
For happy wedlock hours.

 Lor.   Who comes with her? 32
 Mes. None, but a holy hermit and her maid.
I pray you, is my master yet return'd?

 Lor. He is not, nor we have not heard from him.
But go we in, I pray thee, Jessica,   36
And ceremoniously let us prepare
Some welcome for the mistress of the house.

Enter Clown.

 Clo. Sola, sola! wo ha, ho! sola, sola!
 Lor. Who calls?   40
 Clo. Sola! did you see Master Lorenzo?
Master Lorenzo! sola, sola!
 Lor. Leave holloing, man; here.
 Clo. Sola! where? where?   44
 Lor. Here.

31 crosses: *those along the roadside* 39 sola: *imitating the post horn*
41, 42 *Cf. n.*

Clo. Tell him there's a post come from my
master, with his horn full of good news: my
master will be here ere morning.   [*Exit.*] 48
   Lor. Sweet soul, let's in, and there expect their
      coming.
And yet no matter; why should we go in?
My friend Stephano, signify, I pray you,
Within the house, your mistress is at hand;   52
And bring your music forth into the air.

                              [*Exit Stephano.*]

How sweet the moonlight sleeps upon this bank!
Here will we sit, and let the sounds of music
Creep in our ears; soft stillness and the night   56
Become the touches of sweet harmony.
Sit, Jessica: look, how the floor of heaven
Is thick inlaid with patines of bright gold:
There's not the smallest orb which thou behold'st   60
But in his motion like an angel sings,
Still quiring to the young-eyed cherubins;
Such harmony is in immortal souls;
But, whilst this muddy vesture of decay   64
Doth grossly close it in, we cannot hear it.

                  [*Enter Musicians.*]

Come, ho! and wake Diana with a hymn:
With sweetest touches pierce your mistress' ear,
And draw her home with music.   68
   Jes. I am never merry when I hear sweet music.

                              Play music.

   Lor. The reason is, your spirits are attentive:
For do but note a wild and wanton herd,
Or race of youthful and unhandled colts,   72

49 expect: *await*   51 signify: *make it known*
58, 59 the floor of heaven, etc.; *cf. n.*
59 patines: *thin plates, used in celebration of the Eucharist*
62 quiring: *singing in harmony*   70 attentive: *absorbed, concentrated*

Fetching mad bounds, bellowing and neighing loud,
Which is the hot condition of their blood;
If they but hear perchance a trumpet sound,
Or any air of music touch their ears,   76
You shall perceive them make a mutual stand,
Their savage eyes turn'd to a modest gaze
By the sweet power of music: therefore the poet
Did feign that Orpheus drew trees, stones, and floods;
Since nought so stockish, hard, and full of rage,   81
But music for the time doth change his nature.
The man that hath no music in himself,
Nor is not mov'd with concord of sweet sounds,   84
Is fit for treasons, stratagems, and spoils;
The motions of his spirit are dull as night,
And his affections dark as Erebus:
Let no such man be trusted.   Mark the music.   88

Enter Portia and Nerissa [at a distance].

Por. That light we see is burning in my hall.
How far that little candle throws his beams!
So shines a good deed in a naughty world.
    Ner. When   the moon shone, we did not see the
        candle.   92
    Por. So doth the greater glory dim the less:
A substitute shines brightly as a king
Until a king be by, and then his state
Empties itself, as doth an inland brook   96
Into the main of waters.   Music! hark!   *Muisc.*
    Ner. It is your music, madam, of the house.
    Por. Nothing is good, I see, without respect:
Methinks it sounds much sweeter than by day.   100
    Ner. Silence bestows that virtue on it, madam.
    Por. The crow doth sing as sweetly as the lark

87 Erebus: *mythological dark place under Earth*
99 respect: *regard to circumstances*

When neither is attended, and I think
The nightingale, if she should sing by day,   104
When every goose is cackling, would be thought
No better a musician than the wren.
How many things by season season'd are
To their right praise and true perfection!   108
Peace, ho! the moon sleeps with Endymion,
And would not be awak'd!   *Music ceases.*

   Lor.   That is the voice,
Or I am much deceiv'd, of Portia.

   Por. He knows me, as the blind man knows the
   cuckoo,   112
By the bad voice.

   Lor.   Dear lady, welcome home.

   Por. We have been praying for our husbands' wel-
   fare,
Which speed, we hope, the better for our words.
Are they return'd?

   Lor.   Madam, they are not yet;   116
But there is come a messenger before,
To signify their coming.

   Por.   Go in, Nerissa:
Give order to my servants that they take
No note at all of our being absent hence;   120
Nor you, Lorenzo; Jessica, nor you.

                    A tucket sounds.

   Lor. Your husband is at hand; I hear his trumpet:
We are no tell-tales, madam; fear you not.

   Por. This night methinks is but the daylight sick;
It looks a little paler: 'tis a day,   125
Such as the day is when the sun is hid.

103 attended: *given attention*
107 by . . . season'd: *by proper time matured*
109 Endymion: *Selene, the Moon, saw him asleep and loved him*
121 S. d. tucket: *toccata, a flourish on trumpets*

*Enter Bassanio, Antonio, Gratiano, and their
Followers.*

Bass. We should hold day with the Antipodes,
If you would walk in absence of the sun.   128
  Por. Let me give light, but let me not be light;
For a light wife doth make a heavy husband,
And never be Bassanio so for me:
But God sort all! You are welcome home, my lord. 132
  Bass. I thank you, madam. Give welcome to my
      friend:
This is the man, this is Antonio,
To whom I am so infinitely bound.
  Por. You should in all sense be much bound to him,
For, as I hear, he was much bound for you.   137
  Ant. No more than I am well acquitted of.
  Por. Sir, you are very welcome to our house:
It must appear in other ways than words,   140
Therefore I scant this breathing courtesy.
  Gra. [*To Nerissa.*] By yonder moon I swear you do
      me wrong;
In faith, I gave it to the judge's clerk:
Would he were gelt that had it, for my part,   144
Since you do take it, love, so much at heart.
  Por. A quarrel, ho, already! what's the matter?
  Gra. About a hoop of gold, a paltry ring
That she did give me, whose poesy was   148
For all the world like cutlers' poetry
Upon a knife, 'Love me, and leave me not.'
  Ner. What talk you of the posy, or the value?
You swore to me, when I did give it you,   152
That you would wear it till your hour of death,

127, 128 *Cf. n.*   132 sort: *dispose*
141 breathing courtesy: *words of welcome*
148 poesy: *posy on inside of ring*
150 Upon a knife: *they put mottoes on knives*   151 What: *why*

And that it should lie with you in your grave:
Though not for me, yet for your vehement oaths,
You should have been respective and have kept it.　156
Gave it a judge's clerk! no, God's my judge,
The clerk will ne'er wear hair on's face that had it.

　　Gra. He will, an if he live to be a man.

　　Ner. Ay, if a woman live to be a man.　　160

　　Gra. Now, by this hand, I gave it to a youth,
A kind of boy, a little scrubbed boy,
No higher than thyself, the judge's clerk.
A prating boy, that begg'd it as a fee:　　164
I could not for my heart deny it him.

　　Por. You were to blame,—I must be plain with
　　　you,—
To part so slightly with your wife's first gift;
A thing stuck on with oaths upon your finger,　168
And riveted so with faith unto your flesh.
I gave my love a ring and made him swear
Never to part with it; and here he stands.
I dare be sworn for him he would not leave it　172
Nor pluck it from his finger for the wealth
That the world masters.　Now, in faith, Gratiano,
You give your wife too unkind a cause of grief:
An 'twere to me, I should be mad at it.　　176

　　Bass. [*Aside.*] Why, I were best to cut my left hand
　　　off,
And swear I lost the ring defending it.

　　Gra. My Lord Bassanio gave his ring away
Unto the judge that begg'd it, and indeed　　180
Deserv'd it too; and then the boy, his clerk,
That took some pains in writing, he begg'd mine;
And neither man nor master would take aught

---

156 respective: *considerate, careful*
162 scrubbed: *stunted*
174 masters: *owns*

172 leave: *give up*
176 be mad: *run mad*

But the two rings.

    Por.   What ring gave you, my lord? 184
Not that, I hope, which you receiv'd of me.

    Bass. If I could add a lie unto a fault,
I would deny it; but you see my finger
Hath not the ring upon it; it is gone.   188

    Por. Even so void is your false heart of truth.
By heaven, I will ne'er come in your bed
Until I see the ring.

    Ner.   Nor I in yours,
Till I again see mine.

    Bass.   Sweet Portia,   192
If you did know to whom I gave the ring,
If you did know for whom I gave the ring,
And would conceive for what I gave the ring,
And how unwillingly I left the ring,   196
When naught would be accepted but the ring,
You would abate the strength of your displeasure.

    Por. If you had known the virtue of the ring,
Or half her worthiness that gave the ring,   200
Or your own honour to contain the ring,
You would not then have parted with the ring.
What man is there so much unreasonable,
If you had pleas'd to have defended it   204
With any terms of zeal, wanted the modesty
To urge the thing held as a ceremony?
Nerissa teaches me what to believe:
I'll die for 't but some woman had the ring.   208

    Bass. No, by my honour, madam, by my soul,
No woman had it; but a civil doctor,
Which did refuse three thousand ducats of me,
And begg'd the ring, the which I did deny him,   212

---

201 contain: *retain*   205 wanted the: *who would have so wanted*
206 To: *as to*   ceremony: *anything held sacred*
210 civil doctor: *doctor of civil law*

And suffer'd him to go displeas'd away;
Even he that did uphold the very life
Of my dear friend.   What should I say, sweet lady?
I was enforc'd to send it after him;   216
I was beset with shame and courtesy;
My honour would not let ingratitude
So much besmear it.   Pardon me, good lady,
For, by these blessed candles of the night,   220
Had you been there, I think you would have begg'd
The ring of me to give the worthy doctor.

  Por. Let not that doctor e'er come near my house.
Since he hath got the jewel that I lov'd,   224
And that which you did swear to keep for me,
I will become as liberal as you;
I'll not deny him anything I have;
No, not my body, nor my husband's bed.   228
Know him I shall, I am well sure of it:
Lie not a night from home; watch me like Argus:
If you do not, if I be left alone,
Now by mine honour, which is yet mine own,   232
I'll have that doctor for my bedfellow.

  Ner. And I his clerk; therefore be well advis'd
How you do leave me to mine own protection.

  Gra. Well, do you so: let not me take him, then; 236
For if I do, I'll mar the young clerk's pen.

  Ant. I am the unhappy subject of these quarrels.

  Por. Sir, grieve not you; you are welcome notwith-
        standing.

  Bass. Portia, forgive me this enforced wrong;   240
And in the hearing of these many friends,
I swear to thee, even by thine own fair eyes,
Wherein I see myself,—

  Por.   Mark you but that!

217 shame . . . courtesy: *shame at trespassing against good manners*
219 besmear: *soil*   229 well: *very*   230 Argus: *he had a hundred eyes*

In both my eyes he doubly sees himself;   244
In each eye, one: swear by your double self,
And there's an oath of credit.

Bass.   Nay, but hear me:
Pardon this fault, and by my soul I swear
I never more will break an oath with thee.   248

Ant. I once did lend my body for his wealth,
Which, but for him that had your husband's ring,
Had quite miscarried: I dare be bound again,
My soul upon the forfeit, that your lord   252
Will never more break faith advisedly.

Por. Then you shall be his surety. Give him this,
And bid him keep it better than the other.

Ant. Here, Lord Bassanio; swear to keep this ring.

Bass. By heaven! it is the same I gave the doctor!

Por. I had it of him: pardon me, Bassanio,
For, by this ring, the doctor lay with me.

Ner. And pardon me, my gentle Gratiano;   260
For that same scrubbed boy, the doctor's clerk,
In lieu of this last night did lie with me.

Gra. Why, this is like the mending of highways
In summer, where the ways are fair enough.   264
What! are we cuckolds ere we have deserv'd it?

Por. Speak not so grossly. You are all amaz'd:
Here is a letter; read it at your leisure;
It comes from Padua, from Bellario: 268
There you shall find that Portia was the doctor,
Nerissa, there, her clerk: Lorenzo here
Shall witness I set forth as soon as you
And even but now return'd; I have not yet   272
Enter'd my house. Antonio, you are welcome;
And I have better news in store for you

245 double: *full of duplicity*
249 wealth: *welfare*   253 advisedly: *deliberately*

Than you expect: unseal this letter soon;
There you shall find three of your argosies   276
Are richly come to harbour suddenly.
You shall not know by what strange accident
I chanced on this letter.

    Ant.   I am dumb.

    Bass. Were you the doctor and I knew you not?   280

    Gra. Were you the clerk that is to make me cuckold?

    Ner. Ay; but the clerk that never means to do it,
Unless he live until he be a man.

    Bass. Sweet doctor, you shall be my bedfellow: 284
When I am absent, then lie with my wife.

    Ant. Sweet lady, you have given me life and living;
For here I read for certain that my ships
Are safely come to road.

    Por.   How now, Lorenzo!   288
My clerk hath some good comforts too for you.

    Ner. Ay, and I'll give them him without a fee.
There do I give to you and Jessica,
From the rich Jew, a special deed of gift,   292
After his death, of all he dies possess'd of.

    Lor. Fair ladies, you drop manna in the way
Of starved people.

    Por.   It is almost morning,
And yet I am sure you are not satisfied   296
Of these events at full.   Let us go in;
And charge us there upon inter'gatories,
And we will answer all things faithfully.

    Gra. Let it be so: the first inter'gatory   300
That my Nerissa shall be sworn on is,
Whether till the next night she had rather stay,
Or go to bed now, being two hours to day:

---

286 living: *means of life*   288 road: *harbor*
296, 297 satisfied . . . at full: *fully informed*
298 charge . . . upon inter'gatories: *question us on oath*

But were the day come, I should wish it dark, 304
That I were couching with the doctor's clerk.
Well, while I live I'll fear no other thing
So sore as keeping safe Nerissa's ring. *Exeunt.*

306 fear: *concern myself over*

FINIS.

NOTES

Dramatis Personæ. These were first given, under the heading of 'The Actors Names,' in the third Quarto (1637). Words in brackets have been added by later editors.

I. i. 98. *damn those ears*, etc. If they did speak, the people hearing them would immediately call them fools, and thus be in danger of damnation. An allusion to Matthew 5. 22: 'whosoever shall say to his brother . . . Thou fool, shall be in danger of hell fire.'

I. i. 112. *In a neat's tongue dried,* etc. A neat is a bovine animal. The meaning of the whole passage is that everybody ought to talk except prudes. Possibly it is a fragment of some popular saying or song.

I. i. 122. *That.* The word may refer to either the lady or the pilgrimage; it is impossible to say which, but both are probably implied.

I. i. 146. *innocence.* Furness is probably right in thinking innocence here to mean foolishness. Compare the words in the preceding line, 'childhood proof.' Bassanio knew that he had no good reason for asking for more money, when he had not paid what he already owed.

I. i. 167. *Cato's daughter, Brutus' Portia.* The Portia of Brutus appears in Shakespeare's *Julius Caesar,* a play which seems not to have been written till half a dozen years after *The Merchant of Venice.*

I. i. 172. *Colchos' strond.* Colchis was a legendary country in Asia, on the eastern shore (strond) of the Black Sea. Jason went thither in search of the golden fleece, and with the aid of Medea (whom he later deserted) found and brought away the prize.

I. ii. 50. *choose.* This much discussed passage seems to me to mean simply, 'if you don't like me, choose somebody else; choose for yourself.'

I. ii. 74. *he hath neither Latin, French, nor Italian.* Englishmen being, then as now, notorious for their ignorance of other languages. Many believe that Shakespeare would not have written this passage if he had been himself thus ignorant; but the criticism is playful, as that about the Englishman's clothes a few lines below.

I. ii. 87. *the Frenchman became his surety.* A characteristic English gibe at the consistent but half-hearted way in which the French sided with the Scots in their frequent quarrels with the English. In the Folio (1623) the 'Scottish lord' of line 82 is called simply the 'other lord,' to avoid irritating the Scotch King James, who had become King of England in the interval since the play was first produced.

I. ii. 114. *Sibylla.* The Cumaean Sibyl. Apollo promised her that her years should equal the number of grains of sand she held in her hand.

I. ii. 133. *The four strangers.* Six have been definitely mentioned, but Shakespeare was careless of minor consistencies.

I. iii. 35. *the Nazarite.* Commentators have charged Shakespeare with error in applying this word to Christ, since Nazarene is the ordinary term for 'man of Nazareth.' Nazarite is properly the name of an Old Testament Jewish sect who vowed 'to separate themselves unto the Lord' (Numbers 6. 2); but the distinction between Nazarite and Nazarene was not always observed. The allusion in the word 'habitation' is of course to the transfer of the devils from two men into a herd of swine (Matthew 8. 28 ff.).

I. iii. 85. *peel'd me.* 'Me' is here the 'ethical dative,' which is frequent in Shakespeare, but nearly impossible to render in modern English. It slightly stresses the speaker's interest in the action of the verb, but does not otherwise affect the meaning of the sentence and would be omitted in a paraphrase.

I. iii. 144. *Bass.* The Folios and first two Quartos give this speech to Bassanio, and are followed by most editors. The third Quarto (an authority of little importance) gives it to Antonio, which seems inherently better. Antonio is carrying on the dialogue with Shylock; furthermore, Bassanio would not be quite a gentleman if he showed any eagerness here to have the loan made. Shakespeare seldom makes a mistake in delicacy of feeling.

II. i. 7. *whose blood is reddest.* Even then 'red-blooded' was used as it is now.

II. i. 11, 12. *I would not change this hue, Except to steal your thoughts.* The only thing that would induce me to change my bronze skin for white would be the chance of winning you if I were fair.

II. ii. 18. *my father did something smack, something grow to, he had a kind of taste.* This means that his father had sensual tastes. Editors explain 'grow to' as a household phrase applied to burnt milk. Launcelot, however, is speaking with relish.

II. ii. 24. *God bless the mark!* A deprecatory expression, usually 'God save the mark!' It may have had its origin in Ezekiel 9. 6, where the Lord says: 'Slay utterly old and young, both maids, and little children, and women; but come not near any man upon whom is the mark.' Or it may refer to the mark of Cain, Genesis 4. 15: 'And the Lord said unto him, Therefore whosoever slayeth Cain, vengeance shall be taken on him sevenfold. And the Lord set a mark upon Cain, lest any finding him should kill him.'

II. ii. 28. *the very devil incarnation.* The spurious Quarto of 1619 (falsely dated 1600) substitutes 'incarnall' for 'incarnation,' a change very generally adopted by editors who assumed that quarto to be the genuine first edition of the play. Launcelot's 'devil incarnation' blunderingly confuses three different phrases: devil incarnate, devil's incarnation, and devil in carnation (*i.e.*, pink).

II. ii. 37. *being more than sand-blind, high-gravel blind.* Launcelot humorously makes sand-blind a kind of positive to the comparative gravel-blind and superlative stone-blind. 'High-gravel blind' is of course his own invention.

II. ii. 47. *By God's sonties.* A corrupted oath: God's saints, or sanctities (or possibly from the French *santé*).

II. ii. 61, 62. *But I pray you, ergo, old man, ergo, I beseech you, talk you of young Master Launcelot?* Since you address me respectfully as 'your worship,' and Launcelot is my friend and equal, therefore (*ergo*) is it not *Master* Launcelot that you talk of?

II. ii. 102. *what a beard hast thou got!* 'Stage tradition, not improbably from the time of Shakespeare himself, makes Launcelot, at this point, kneel with his back to the sand-blind old Father, who, of course, mistakes his long back hair for a beard, of which his face is perfectly innocent.' (Staunton.)

II. ii. 116. *you may tell every finger I have with my ribs.* Topsy-turvy nonsense for 'you may count every rib with your finger.'

II. ii. 164. *The old proverb is very well parted.* The proverb was: 'God's grace is gear enough.' Parted means distributed, divided.

II. ii. 174. *table,* etc. Palmistry. Table was the technical term for the palm of the hand. As Launcelot opens his hand to inspect the palm, the action suggests to him the idea of laying the hand on the book (Bible) to swear an oath. 'A simple (moderate) line of life' (l. 176) is used humorously for the reverse. Compare 'a small trifle of wives,' 'a simple coming-in for one man' (l. 178). The number of wives was supposed to be indicated by the number of lines running from the ball of the thumb towards the line of life.

II. v. 43. *worth a Jewess' eye.* Alluding to a common proverb, 'worth a Jew's eye.' The early editions spell the word 'Iewes' and modern editors find it difficult to decide whether Jewess' or Jew's is intended.

II. vi. 15. *scarfed.* Most editors think this refers to flag-decorations. I believe it alludes simply to the spread of sails, which are fresh and strong at the beginning of the voyage, and at the return home are 'ragged . . . Lean, rent, and beggar'd.'

II. ix. 85. *what would my lord?* It is generally explained that Portia says this playfully to the servant-messenger. Possibly she supposes, however, from the servant's excited manner that Arragon has returned for some reason, and so makes this impatient query.

III. i. 30. *the wings she flew withal.* That is, the boy's dress that was the means of her escape.

III. i. 99. *Why thou—* Furness and many other editors believe 'thou' to be a misprint for 'then' (which is actually the reading of the second Folio). But surely Shylock is going to call Jessica a bad name, and either checks himself or can't think of one bad enough.

III. i. 115. *Where? in Genoa?* The early editions all have 'here in Genoa,' though Shylock is speaking in Venice. Rowe introduced the emendation, which has been accepted in most modern editions. Furness, however, justifies the original reading by the reasoning that in contrast with rumors of far-off losses on the Goodwins, etc., a loss confirmed in Genoa seems very near and definite.

III. ii. 20, 21. *Prove it so, Let fortune go to hell for it, not I.* Should it prove, by the lottery of the caskets, that I am not yours, let chance bear the blame (which could not be adequately punished short of hell), not me.

III. ii. 54, 55. *With no less presence, but with much more love, Than young Alcides.* Because Alcides

(Hercules) rescued Hesione from the sea-monster, not for love but for the horses promised him by her father Laomedon, King of Troy. Portia compares herself to Hesione in the words, 'I stand for sacrifice' (l. 57). The 'Dardanian wives' (l. 58) are the Trojan matrons.

III. ii. 94. *Upon supposed fairness.* This may mean 'on the strength of their fictitious beauty,' as some believe; but the beauty of the hair is real, not fictitious. The phrase probably refers rather to the 'supposed fairness' of the head that the locks adorn, which is really not fair at all.

III. ii. 99. *Veiling an Indian beauty.* This is regarded as a very difficult passage, but why? Bassanio has been talking about lovely golden false hair adorning an ugly head, hence concealing it too. Thus the 'beauteous scarf Veiling an Indian beauty' means the fair veil concealing a black, that is loathsome, beauty. The emphasis is on the word 'Indian,' not 'beauty.'

III. ii. 112. *In measure rain thy joy.* The verb is certainly rain, not rein, as some critics have taken it. The meaning is: Pour thy joy moderately.

III. ii. 200, 201. *You lov'd, I lov'd; for intermission No more pertains to me, my lord, than you.* There has been much dispute over the meaning of these lines, all due to the punctuation of the early editions, which unanimously omit the semicolon after 'I lov'd' and insert a comma (or period) after 'intermission.' If the old punctuation is retained and understood to mark the logical relations of the parts of the sentence, the best explanation of line 200 would be to interpret 'intermission' as meaning comedy, like 'interlude.' You loved in the style of high drama, I match you with love less dignified perhaps, but real: I am to you as farce to drama. This, however, would leave line 201 far from clear; and it is much more likely that the pointing of the old editions is a striking instance of the tendency in Shakespeare's time to punctuate rhetori-

cally instead of logically. The comma after 'intermission' would thus mark the drop of the actor's voice,
not the close of a clause in the sentence.

III. ii. 220. *Salanio*. The original editions give the
name as Salerio here and throughout the rest of the
scene, and several of the most important modern editors, on the strength of this, include Salerio, as well as
Salanio and Salarino, among the characters in the play.
It is highly unlikely that Shakespeare intended to add
this third unnecessary character for the purposes of a
single scene: Salerio may be either a slip of the author's
pen or a blunder of the compositor.

III. iv. 20. *the semblance of my soul*. Antonio,
whose likeness to Bassanio makes him also like the very
soul of Portia.

III. iv. 53. *Unto the tranect, to the common ferry*.
The meaning of tranect, evidently an uncommon word,
is purposely explained in the words that follow. Since
no other example of 'tranect' has been found, Rowe,
followed by most modern editors, substitutes 'traject,'
which is taken to be an anglicized version of 'tra-
ghetto,' the contemporary name of the Venetian ferries.

III. v. 20. *I shall be saved by my husband*. See 1
Corinthians 7. 14: 'For the unbelieving husband is
sanctified by the wife, and the unbelieving wife is
sanctified by the husband.'

III. v. 57. *'cover' is the word*. Launcelot here
means by cover 'bring the meal to the table.' In his
next speech (l. 60) he quibbles on another meaning,
'put on one's hat,' which it would be undutiful for him,
a servant, to do in the presence of Lorenzo.

III. v. 83. *mean it*. Either, 'do not mean to lead
an upright life,' or 'do not observe a mean (temperance,
moderation).'

IV. i. 56. *a woollen bagpipe*. Covered with woollen
cloth. Among the many unnecessary emendations for

'woollen' which have been suggested are swollen, wooden, and wauling (cf. caterwauling). The last is the most plausible.

IV. i. 73, 74. *You may as well use question with the wolf, Why he hath made the ewe bleat for the lamb.* An accident in the preparation of the First Quarto caused the omission of the first three words in line 73 and the first four in line 74 in certain copies of that edition. The Folio text was set up from one of the defective copies.

IV. i. 118. *Than to live still, and write mine epitaph.* Compare Hamlet to Horatio (*Hamlet*, V. ii. 361-363):

'Absent thee from felicity awhile,
 And in this harsh world draw thy breath in pain,
 To tell my story.'

IV. i. 129. *And for thy life let justice be accus'd.* Possibly meaning that justice is wrong for allowing him to live at all; but I think it means that justice should be condemned for allowing him to live in his present purpose, which though horrible is quite legal.

IV. i. 149. *Bellario's letter.* Many say that Bellario had told Portia how to circumvent Shylock; but this is not only an unnecessary supposition, it spoils the scene. If Portia did not use her mother-wit here, why not let Bellario go himself and thus have Portia run no risk? Doubtless she had persuaded him to be 'very sick.' The subsequent citation of the law proving Shylock guilty of intent to murder may very well have come from Bellario.

IV. i. 223. *A Daniel come to judgment.* *I.e.*, a just young judge has arisen. The allusion is to the History of Susanna in the Apocrypha: 'the Lord raised up the holy spirit of a young youth, whose name was Daniel,' and who proceeded to give righteous judgment where his elders had blundered.

V. i. 41, 42. *Master Lorenzo? Master Lorenzo!* The only two authoritative texts, those of the First

Quarto (1600) and First Folio, both print these words, 'M. Lorenzo & M. Lorenzo,' which may be intended for 'Master Lorenzo and Mistress Lorenzo' (*i.e.*, Jessica).

V. i. 58, 59. *the floor of heaven Is thick inlaid with patines of bright gold.* Shakespeare may have forgotten that on a bright, moonlight night one cannot see many stars. Furness, however, suggests that the 'patines' are not stars, but bits of illuminated cloud.

V. i. 127, 128. *We should hold day with the Antipodes, If you would walk in absence of the sun.* With you to replace the sun in the night we should think that our day, as it is on the other side of the globe; *i.e.*, you would turn night to day and outshine the sun.

APPENDIX A

SOURCES OF THE PLAY

It is usually said that there are two separate stories in this play: the Pound of Flesh story, and the story of the Three Caskets. But Professor R. G. Moulton in his admirable book, *Shakespeare as a Dramatic Artist,* emphasizes the fact that there are four strands in the plot, the Pound of Flesh, the Three Caskets, the Elopement of Jessica and Lorenzo and the Episode of the Rings. He points out cleverly and perhaps fancifully the exact moment when Shakespeare brings all four elements together.

There was an old ballad of Gernutus, printed in Percy's *Reliques* (1765), which gives the pound of flesh incident in detail. The difficulty is that no one can prove whether this ballad preceded Shakespeare's *Merchant,* and may thus be considered a source, or followed hard upon the appearance of the play, and is thus merely a tribute to its popularity. The chief source is probably an Italian work, *Il Pecorone,* written in 1378 by Giovanni Fiorentino, and published in 1565. No English translation of this is extant; but as Elizabethan England was familiar with a very large number of vernacular translations from the Italian, it is probable that Shakespeare had access to one in this instance. *Il Pecorone* is a collection of tales, and one of them has the story of a rich woman at Belmont, who is eventually married to a young gentleman, whose friend, in order to lend him money, had come within the danger of an avaricious Jew, who demanded as surety a pound of flesh. The situation is saved by the lady in the court room, who obtains her marriage ring with subsequent pleasantries. The Jew story, however, was a common one in all European literatures.

The Caskets story appears in the *Gesta Romanorum,* a collection of tales dating in England from the thirteenth century. Its editor, Herrtage, describes it as a 'collection of fictitious narratives in Latin, compiled from Oriental apologues, monkish legends, classical stories, tales of chroniclers, popular traditions, and other sources, which it would be now difficult and perhaps impossible to discover.' An English translation was well known in Shakespeare's day, and this book may have been the source of the Caskets plot in *The Merchant of Venice.*

Shakespeare may have invented the Lorenzo-Jessica love story; some think he obtained it from a tale by Massuccio di Salerno, *cir.* 1470, but I doubt it.

In addition to these probable and possible sources, Gosson, in his *Schoole of Abuse* (1579), mentions a play acted at the Bull Inn, called *The Jew.* From his brief description of it, many editors have been convinced that this drama is the prototype of Shakespeare's play, and the real source; but as no copy of it has yet been found, all statements concerning it are largely conjecture.

Shakespeare was undoubtedly influenced by Marlowe's tragedy of blood, *The Jew of Malta,* which was written sometime between 1589 and 1593, and was immensely popular, as it deserved to be. This Jew was a monster rather than a human being; but he was certainly the most famous Jew on the Elizabethan stage until the first matinée of *The Merchant of Venice.* His daughter similarly loves a Christian youth, throws down moneybags from a balcony at night, and ultimately flees from home; and her father's combination of parental and financial emotion infallibly suggests Shylock's ejaculations.

Dr. Johnson, as quoted by Furness, made an epitome of *Il Pecorone,* from which the following extracts are here given (Giannetto=Bassanio; Ansaldo=Antonio):

'Poor Giannetto's head was day and night full of
the thoughts of his bad success. When Ansaldo in-
quired what was the matter, he confessed he could never
be contented till he should be in a condition to regain
all that he had lost. When Ansaldo found him resolved, he began to sell everything he had to furnish
this other fine ship with merchandise; but as he wanted
still ten thousand ducats, he applied himself to a Jew
at Mestri, and borrowed them on condition that if they
were not paid on the feast of St. John in the next
month of June, the Jew might take a pound of flesh
from any part of his body he pleased. . . .

'Giannetto governed excellently, and caused justice
to be administered impartially. . . . But one day, as
he stood at the window of the palace with his bride,
he saw a number of people pass along the piazza, with
lighted torches in their hands. What is the meaning
of this? said he. The lady answered, They are artifi-
cers going to make their offerings at the Church of St.
John, this day being his festival. Giannetto instantly
recollected Ansaldo, gave a great sigh, and turned
pale. . . . The lady told him to mount on horseback,
and go by land the nearest way, to take some attendants, and an hundred thousand ducats; and not to
stop until he arrived at Venice. . . .

'. . . The lady now arrives in Venice, in her
lawyer's dress. . . . Giannetto proposed to the Jew
to apply to this lawyer. With all my heart, says the
Jew; but let who will come, I will stick to my bond.
They came to this judge and saluted him. Giannetto
did not remember him; for he had disguised his face
with the juice of certain herbs. Giannetto and the Jew
each told the merits of the cause to the judge; who,
when he had taken the bond and read it, said to the
Jew, I must have you take the hundred thousand
ducats, and release this honest man, who will always
have a grateful sense of the favour done to him. The

Jew replied, I will do no such thing. The judge answered, it will be better for you. The Jew was positive to yield nothing. Upon this they go to the tribunal appointed for such judgments; and our judge says to the Jew, Do you cut a pound of this man's flesh where you choose. The Jew ordered him to be stripped naked; and takes in his hand a razor, which had been made on purpose. Giannetto seeing this, turning to the judge, This, says he, is not the favour I asked of you. Be quiet, says he, the pound of flesh is not yet cut off. As soon as the Jew was going to begin, Take care what you do, says the judge, if you take more or less than a pound, I will order your head to be struck off; and beside, if you shed one drop of blood you shall be put to death.' [Then follows the discomfiture of the Jew, who finding that he cannot get even the principal of the loan, tears up the bond in a rage, receiving no further punishment. The judge declines to accept any money from Giannetto, but succeeds in inducing him to give her the ring, whereupon follow the now familiar complications. Giannetto wept when his lady pretended that he had been unfaithful; reconciliation followed, and they lived happily forever after.]

For the original of the Caskets story, the following extracts are given from the *Gesta Romanorum,* as printed in Furness.

'Then was the emperour right glad of her safety and comming, and had great compassion on her, saying: Ah faire lady, for the love of my sonne thou hast suffered much woe, neverthelesse if thou be worthie to be his wife, soone shall I prove.

'And when he had thus said, he commanded to bring forth three vessels, the first was made of pure gold, beset with precious stones without, and within full of dead mens bones, and thereupon was ingraven this

posey: Whoso chooseth me shall finde that he de-
serveth.

'The second vessel was made of fine silver, filled with
earth and wormes, and the superscription was thus:
Whoso chooseth me shall finde that his nature desireth.

'The third vessel was made of lead, full within
of precious stones, and the superscription, Whoso
chooseth me shall finde that God hath disposed to him.'

But whatever incidents Shakespeare may or may not
have drawn from sources, the oftener one compares his
play with these stories, the greater seems his genius.
His characters are complex human beings; and the
speech of Portia on mercy is only one of the evidences
of the richness of the mind and character whence it
came.

Shylock is a man as well as a Jew; and while Shakespeare took the national attitude toward Jews, and
wished his readers and the spectators to rejoice in
Shylock's discomfiture, he allowed Shylock to state his
own case fairly, and in his comparison of himself with
Christians, to reveal his human feelings. It is absurd
to suppose that Shakespeare intended Shylock to be a
hero, or to carry the sympathy of the audience; on the
other hand, Shakespeare was not writing anti-Semitic
propaganda, but a play for the theatre, in which the
interest is immensely heightened by making every
character a recognizable human being.

APPENDIX B

The History of the Play

It is generally believed that *The Merchant of Venice* was written between 1594 and 1598; but all we know is that it was written before 1598. In that year Francis Meres published his *Palladis Tamia*, where, in a comparison of English poets with the classics, he mentions Shakespeare as a leading contemporary dramatist, and in the list of his productions gives *Merchant of Venice*.

Henslowe's Diary, under date of 25 August, 1594, shows that a new play which he describes as 'the Venesyon comodey,' was performed. No one can prove that this is a reference to the *Merchant of Venice*. Inasmuch as most editors and critics delight in conjecture, it is surprising that no one has tried to prove that this is a play wherein Shakespeare dramatizes his adventures with the 'Venison' of Sir Thomas Lucy, of Charlecote Park.

A quarto edition was printed in 1600, and upon this the Folio text of 1623 was based. In 1619 a spurious edition, bearing the false date 1600, was foisted upon the world. Till 1906 it was generally regarded as the earliest edition and allowed vastly more authority than it in fact deserves.

No one knows when the play was first performed. A version by George Granville, Viscount Lansdowne, was played at London in 1701, and 'held the stage for exactly forty years.' It is printed in Furness as a literary curiosity.

Of the famous actors who have interpreted Shylock, Richard Burbage, the Elizabethan star, may have been the first. In 1741, Charles Macklin, an Irishman, restored the Shakespearean version to the stage, for which he should receive everlasting credit. When he was nearly a hundred years old, he made his last appearance in the rôle of Shylock. The next great actor to take the part was Edmund Kean, in 1814, whose original interpretation made a powerful impression.

In the latter part of the nineteenth century, the greatest impersonation was that by Edwin Booth, who displayed all the resources of his genius. In many ways, it was his finest rôle. Henry Irving attracted wide attention by making Shylock a sympathetic character, but he was neither Elizabethan nor particularly impressive. Richard Mansfield, with his uncanny intelligence, gave a memorable presentation, in which the fiendish character of Shylock was predominant, and yet his humanity not lost. Contemporary with him was the great German actor, Ernst von Possart, who made *Der Kaufmann von Venedig* a favorite play with Continental audiences. He was one of the best of all Shylocks. At the present writing (1922) the only important English-speaking actors of the Jew are Edward Sothern, who, with Julia Marlowe as Portia, gives an admirable production; Walter Hampden; and David Warfield.

APPENDIX C

The Text of the Present Edition

The text of the present volume is, by permission, based upon that of the Oxford Shakespeare, compared with the First Folio and Quarto texts. The following changes from the Oxford text have been made:

1. The stage directions are those of the First Folio, necessary additional words being inserted in square brackets.

2. The punctuation has been occasionally altered, and the spelling of a few words normalized; *e.g.*, villainy (villany), nobody (no body), everywhere (every where).

3. The following alterations of text have been introduced, usually in deference to the authority of the genuine (Heyes) Quarto of 1600 (Q) and the First Folio (F). Readings of the present edition precede and those of Craig (Oxford) follow the colon:

I. iii. 80	eanlings which (QF): eanlings that	
	113	spit: spet (QF). Cf. II. vii. 45
	144	*Bass.* (QF): *Ant.*
	162	dealings (QF): dealing (later Folios)
II. ii. 28	incarnation (QF): incarnal (spurious quarto)	
	103	phill-horse (QF): thill-horse (Theobald)
	125	farthest (QF): very furthest
II. ix. 4	stand (QF): stands (misprint?)	
III. i. 50	was used (QF): used (Rowe)	
	90	there, there, there, there! (QF): there there, there!
III. ii. 245	steals (QF): steal (Pope)	
III. iv. 53	tranect (QF): traject (Rowe)	
IV. i. 21	strange apparent (QF): strange-apparent (Walker)	
	56	woollen (QF): wauling (Capell)
	279	but (Q): not (F)
	373	unto (QF): into (misprint?)
V. i. 185	hope, which (QF): hope, that	
	236	let not me (QF): let me not
	302	Whether (QF): Whe'r

APPENDIX D

Suggestions for Collateral Reading

William Hazlitt: *Characters of Shakespear's Plays,* 1817. (Reprinted in Everyman's Library.)

H. H. Furness: *A New Variorum Edition of Shakespeare,* Vol. VII, *The Merchant of Venice,* 1888.

R. G. Moulton: *Shakespeare as a Dramatic Artist,* new ed., 1893. (First published, 1885.)

Charlotte Porter and Helen A. Clarke: 'First Folio' edition of *The Merchant of Venice,* 1905.

Stopford A. Brooke: *On Ten Plays of Shakespeare,* 6th impression, 1919, pp. 127-154.

St. John Ervine: *The Realistic Test of Drama.* 'Yale Review,' Jan., 1922, pp. 288-298. (A discussion of the improbabilities in the plot.)

Raymond M. Alden: *Shakespeare,* 1922, pp. 207-214.

Sir Sidney Lee: *Life of Shakespeare,* new edition, 1922. (First published in 1898.)

INDEX OF WORDS GLOSSED

(Figures in full-faced type refer to page-numbers)